# HOME
## *is where you*
# MAKE IT

# HOME
## *is where you*
# MAKE IT

### DIY Ideas & Styling Secrets to Create a
### Home You Love, Whether You Rent or Own

## GENEVA VANDERZEIL

## TILLER PRESS

NEW YORK LONDON TORONTO SYDNEY NEW DELHI

# About the author

Geneva Vanderzeil is a maker, stylist, and photographer. She grew up in Brisbane, Australia. After moving to London in 2008, Geneva started her first blog, *A Pair & A Spare*, which quickly became one of the most popular websites in the world, with millions of readers and features in several major newspapers and magazines. It was relaunched in 2019 as *Collective Gen*.

With the huge success of the website, Geneva left her day job as a town planner in 2012 and published a book about her favorite DIY fashion projects. She has turned her passion for creativity into a career, cultivating a global community on her site, running workshops and designing product lines.

After living in Hong Kong and traveling the world, Geneva decided it was time to settle down. Never one to take the easy route, she bought a dilapidated cottage in Brisbane and set about completely overhauling it, turning it from a two-bedroom nightmare into a light-filled, three-bedroom home—complete with the maker studio of her dreams. Through this process, a love of interior DIY projects and styling evolved into an all-out addiction. It only made sense to put it all down on paper.

Geneva currently lives in Brisbane with her partner, Ben, and daughter, Frankie.

# Contents

## The Art of Making a Room 11

*Room four*

## The Bedroom 123

MAKE IT A SANCTUARY

*Room five*

## The Closet 155

MAKE IT ORGANIZED

*Room six*

## The Bathroom 173

MAKE IT A RETREAT

*Room seven*

## The Nursery 193

MAKE IT FUN

# The Art
# of Making
# a Room

# Making Your Space Your Own

Over the last few years, and especially since having our daughter Frankie, I've come to truly understand the concept of "home." Not home as a picture-perfect space filled with meticulously planned elements but a retreat from the pace of life outside, somewhere that grounds us and makes us feel truly happy and content. I've experienced a longing to not only spend more time at home but also to make it with my own hands and style it with love, personality, and imagination.

I've been writing this book in my head for a long, long time—since the moment I stepped into our awkward London rental apartment and proceeded to feverishly DIY it into the ultimate retreat. And again, when I walked around our tiny Hong Kong apartment (where we could lie in bed and reach into the kitchen), signed the lease, and over time made it into a space we never wanted to leave. I knew that one day I would have to share this knowledge with you. It's the knowledge that's easy to miss when you're collating Pinterest boards or pulling pages out of a magazine— you don't need to have the perfect space to make a home that's perfect for you. Because home is where you make it.

I know it can be disheartening to try to make something out of an unappealing room—in my time living and renting in Australia, the UK, and Hong Kong, I've seen my fair share of terrible spaces. Add to that the fact that if you flip through Pinterest or read design magazines, it can be easy to think that if you don't have a New York–style loft or a sprawling LA home, it's not even worth trying.

But it's my belief that any space can be made into a beautiful home; not necessarily perfect, but perfect for you. Usually, all it takes is a bit of imagination and a whole lot of elbow grease.

After years of readers and friends asking for tips to deal with the common challenges of making a home welcoming—low lighting, ugly carpet, small spaces, tiny budget—I thought it was time I put everything I've learned and experienced into a book. If you're looking around your space and thinking, "There's no way anyone can make this dump a home," I beg to differ! Pull up a chair, make yourself a cup of tea, and get sucked into this handbook.

Making a home you love is about getting your hands dirty, getting creative, working with what you've got, and, in the end, making your space meaningful, functional, and beautiful. Let this book guide you through how to DIY, style, and perfect your less-than-perfect space. I promise—once you start, you won't look back!

My hope is that you create a space that you can look around and feel proud of, full of handmade touches—a home that's beautiful and unique to you. I hope it can give you the sense of belonging and self that comes with making and creating, and the knowledge that it wasn't that hard.

It can be scary to start tackling projects in the home, and for many of us that means we stall and struggle until we ultimately give up. But in this book, you'll see just how easy, fun, and affordable it is to create each room in your house by hand. You can make a home wherever you are, because home is where you make it.

*Geneva*

# Starting out

Getting creative with spaces, furniture, and styling is in my bones. Ever since I was young I've been addicted to transforming what's in front of me, whether it was a thrift-store dress, a sofa, or a whole space. I blame this on my parents! My mother taught me the art of digging deep in secondhand stores, seeing past all the awful pieces and finding the diamonds in the rough. Every weekend we could be found searching high and low in thrift stores, junk shops, garage sales, and anywhere that one man's trash could become two women's treasures. My father, although not a fan of secondhand stores, was a bit of an inventor and was always tinkering in his shed, searching for new ideas. These two influences powered my creativity and helped me to think outside the box about how I can re-create or make something myself. To this day, my first thought whenever I see something I like is, "How can I make that?" I've found that with some basic skills and a bit of time, you can make so many of the things you love.

Although I've always been creative in every aspect of my life, I have to admit that my first love was fashion. It was on the back of my fashion DIY projects that I started my website and wrote my first book. It was fashion that gave me inspiration to share and reach a community. But as I started investing my creativity in our (quite frankly) awful rental apartments, I wanted to share that, too.

And I have a brilliant partner in crime! Ben, my partner for the past twelve years, is an interior designer, and also the most capable person I've ever met. In his head he carries a seemingly infinite number of answers to any question I have, from designing a house and making furniture to styling a space, matching decor styles, and even picking doorknobs. It's from this fountain of wisdom that I've gleaned much of my technical knowledge about interiors. And it's exactly why I chose to renovate a whole house with him! People warned us about renovating together, but in all honesty (and don't hate me), we didn't have one disagreement in the time that we completely transformed a tiny cottage into a two-story house.

If the prospect of making and styling your own space seems daunting because of your skill level, a perceived lack of imagination, or a worry that you don't know how to style your space, you've come to the right place. In this book I'll show you that not only is it fun to develop a vision for your space, it's incredibly rewarding to DIY and style it so that it's perfect for you.

Renovating an
old, run-down
cottage was one
of the most
incredible, and
challenging,
experiences—
but, in truth,
you're never
really finished
making a space!

# Our renovation

Ben and I have shared the amazing experience of renovating our first house. We bought a crumbling old cottage and were excited to make it our own. The main goal for the architectural design was to keep as many of the original features as possible—the original flooring, the iconic veranda, the tongue-and-groove walls, and the details above the doorways—while also extending and opening up the spaces and adding much-needed light.

In terms of decor, we wanted light, bright spaces in which we could integrate color, but we found ways to do this that weren't too overwhelming, such as adding color to cupboards, cabinets, and doorways. Another major goal was to integrate a range of DIY ideas and hacks—simple updates to off-the-rack items and vintage pieces that made the house feel high-end and unique, without blowing the budget. I'm DIY obsessed, so this was my favorite part!

Our biggest inspiration when styling the space was to mix and match different eras and items to give the house a lived-in and bespoke feel. We mixed rattan, mid-century furniture and industrial pieces so that the house felt like us and not like a showroom. This is something that Ben specializes in, both in residential interior design and in his commercial projects—mixing styles and decor so that a space feels comfortable, cozy, and lived in. In all honesty, I would have included a lot more rattan, but Ben convinced me that a splash of any one type of material has more impact, and he was right.

We're so happy with the end result. I think we've managed to maintain the details of the cottage that we loved so much, while modernizing and meeting our goal of having a really functional house. We don't have a huge yard, which is something I'd love to have one day, but we had to choose between internal and external space, and in the end we chose to lay out the house itself really well.

DIY addict!

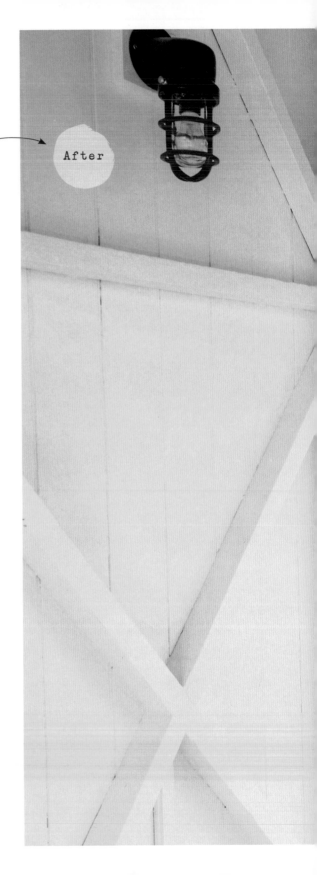

Before

After

Even though we made some big changes to our cottage, we tried to keep as many of the heritage elements as possible, including this amazing bullnose veranda that we love so much! It's now a feature of the house.

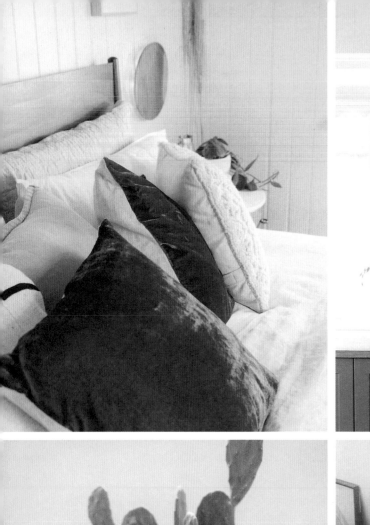

# How to Use This Book

My main goal has been to create a simple handbook that decodes each room for you, providing simple DIY and interior styling advice so that you're able to easily create a home you love, no matter how perfect (or imperfect) your space. Creating a space that's beautiful AND functional can seem daunting, but with a few tips and tricks, you can DIY and style any space like a pro.

First, I'll take you through a six-step process for making a room, working from the ground up so that you know how to tackle a space in a straightforward and cohesive way. When it comes to interiors, failing to plan is planning for failure, so I've boiled it down to give you the foundations of making a room, no matter what it is. Next, I've given you some general DIY and styling advice that applies to any room in any house.

After that, I dive into the different rooms of the house, outlining basic elements to consider for each room, then giving you a few of my favorite DIY projects, as well as a variety of styling tips tailored to the room. I've also included guides for dealing with the key challenges of a less-than-perfect space, because, remember, you don't need to have a perfect space to create something that's perfect for you.

Consider this book your companion to making a space that's a joy to come home to. From learning easy and adaptable DIY skills to styling your spaces, you'll have plenty of tricks in your home-making toolkit. Don't be afraid to experiment with the projects and ideas in this book—once you understand the foundations, you'll be able to use them to make your space uniquely yours.

# Six Steps to Success

What makes a space? Is it the way it looks? How it feels to be in it? Or how it functions? In fact, it's a mix of all of these. The best way to get the space right is to approach the DIY and styling of a room with a method, rather than in a haphazard way. That's not to say that you can't experiment or change the space over time, but it's worth understanding a room and how it works before you dive into redesigning or redecorating it.

## Step 1. Consider the function

A room might look perfect, but if it functions poorly and is uncomfortable, it's not going to be a space where you'll want to spend time. The starting point for any room is to understand what purpose you want it to achieve and what that means for the major elements of the room. Is it all about family time, and therefore needs to include a large sofa? Or is it a bedroom that's used just for sleeping, and so should have only a bed? Write down the function of the room and the key elements you need in it before you start thinking about anything else.

## Step 2. Understand the actual room

It's easy to get distracted by ideas and inspirations and forget about the space in real life. Take a moment to assess the best (and worst) features of the space. Where is the natural light coming from? How does the roofline feel? Where are the passageways through the space? Look at the key features you want to highlight and those you'll need to work around.

## Step 3. Put together a mood board

It's time to start brainstorming and collecting ideas for how you want the space to look. Collect images (either on Pinterest or from magazines) that show the mood and the aesthetics you like in a space. Think about the atmosphere you want to create, as well as the design style you're aiming for. Take into account the room and the function you have in mind when putting together your mood board. There's no point in building a concept that fails to reference the room itself.

I love creating mood boards to help me visualize a space.

*My current favorites*

Mustard    Khaki    Dusty Rose    Sand

## Step 4. Choose a color palette

If you've ever been in a space that didn't work, even though it seemed like it should, it was probably due to the mix of colors. A feeling of haphazardness is often caused by the lack of a color scheme. While color palettes shouldn't be overly prescriptive or bland, having a color palette to refer to—even if it's a flexible one—will help your space evolve cohesively and give it a harmonious feel.

So, where to start? There are lots of ways to choose a color palette for a particular room (or an entire home), but I often use one of the following methods:

* **Use patterns as a guide.** One trick for choosing a color scheme that works together is to look at patterns in which colors can be seen together (and where someone else has done the hard work of matching the tones for you). Once you find a pattern with colors you like, consider how you can translate that into a room. Decide which color you will use as the dominant color and which colors can be added as supporting shades.
* **Use art or imagery for inspiration.** I found inspiration for the color scheme for our renovation in a picture of a yard. The pink walls and green plants in the picture showed me that these colors worked together well, so I set about translating that into the color scheme for the house.

* **Ground it with neutrals.** Once you have some brighter colors in mind, choose some neutrals to bring the whole palette together. I find that neutrals provide the negative space needed to give the brighter colors room to shine. As a starting point, use neutrals for 50 percent of the color scheme.
* **Go minimal.** Although I like color in my space, it's not for everyone. When developing a minimalist color scheme, consider the tones and also the way that other finishes and textures can add interest to the space.

## Step 5. Pick your furniture

The right pieces of furniture will make your space both functional and visually cohesive. Here are a few factors to think about when deciding on furniture.

* **Construction:** Choose furniture that feels solid and durable—avoid pieces made from particle board and light aluminum.
* **Silhouette:** Try to choose furniture that will complement the design of your space but not date too quickly. Classic designs will stand the test of time.
* **Fabric:** Make sure the fabric is appropriate for the amount of use it will get, and choose colors that won't show stains, particularly in a heavily used space like the living room.

## Step 6. Style with the right decor

Once you have all the functional elements of the space in place, it's time to make it your own by adding decor like rugs, plants, books, and table accessories. Good styling is so much more than putting objects on every available surface. The best spaces are styled in ways that are thoughtful and bring the room to life. When in doubt, start with a great rug and add some plants in awkward corners and on shelves. These two elements can completely transform a room. Finish by styling your shelves, tabletops, and cabinets. Don't feel like you have to go overboard, but it's nice to add a few details that bring life and depth to the room.

# The Toolkit

You don't need a mountain of tools and materials (or a shed to store them in) to get started. For me, simple is best! I've deliberately included projects and ideas that require the least amount of tools and materials, focusing on using what you have, finding hacks that make every project easier, and using the same tools and materials time and time again.

Having said that, having a few key tools will open up a huge number of projects to you and make them so much more professional than they would be otherwise. As much as I like homemade, I prefer my projects to look like they were made by someone who knew what they were doing! Most of the tools that I've suggested should fit into a couple of baskets that you can keep in a cupboard and pull out when it's making time.

## Basic toolbox

Get yourself some simple and inexpensive tools that will enable you to complete most simple projects:

* **Hammer**
* **Screwdriver (manual and/or electric)**
* **Pliers**
* **Tape measure**
* **Wire cutters**
* **Staple gun**
* **Clamps**
* **Assorted nails and screws**

I also recommend buying some protective gloves and safety goggles. Other useful items to include in a toolbox are a pencil, ruler, level, square, sandpaper, adhesive tape, sewing needles and pins, and an assortment of paintbrushes.

## Drill

Scared of a drill? Don't be! A drill and a few screws have the potential to instantly take you from novice to professional. Owning and knowing how to use a drill opens up a whole world of DIY possibilities.

When buying a drill, consider the size and weight, whether you want a corded or cordless one, and what bits and screws you'll need for your projects (they differ depending on the material you're drilling). For the projects in this book, you only need to be able to drill into wood, but once you've mastered that, you can experiment with other materials like metal, concrete, and tile.

## Sewing machine

Sewing is one of my great loves, and being able to sew, even with very basic skills, is a huge asset for textile projects that can completely transform the feel of a space. I know that many people feel overwhelmed by the idea of sewing, but it's a skill worth investing in. If you're buying a sewing machine, a basic model will suffice to begin with; you'll find that beginners' projects use mainly straight stitches.

## Glue

Glue is one of the obvious tools in your DIY toolkit, but the glue you use will depend on the project and the materials you're working with.

* **Superglue:** Superglue is great for projects that need a very strong bond. Be careful when you're applying this, as it can easily stick to your skin and is difficult to remove. If you have only one type of glue in your toolkit, make it this one.
* **White glue:** White glue is useful for craft projects, but it takes longer to dry and is more difficult to apply. It's best used to stick down cardboard, paper, and other porous surfaces.

*Upcycling!*

* **A glue gun:** I've always had a love-hate relationship with the humble glue gun. For a long time it signified corner-cutting, but over time I've come to realize that a glue gun is great for projects that need a quick-drying hold.

## Sharp scissors and a craft knife

You'll need some very sharp scissors when working with materials like leather. A sharp craft knife with a retractable blade is also essential for times when you need a more precise cut than you can make with scissors, or when you're making a one-sided cut.

## Fabric

Fabric is an addiction for me, and I'm always stocking up on linens, cottons, and other natural fabrics to use in craft projects. If you haven't yet mastered a sewing machine, you might think you don't need a collection of fabrics, but they're great for upholstering, making curtains, throwing over tables, or draping over furniture. Secondhand stores are a great source for fabrics.

## Rope

There's something organic and rustic about rope, and it lends an expensive feel to any project you use it in. A simple cotton rope is great for most projects, but you can also use jute, sisal, or nylon rope, depending on what you're making. Think about which elements the rope will be exposed to. For example, nylon rope is better for outdoor projects that will be exposed to the rain.

## Leather

I love using leather. It's a seriously versatile material that has the power to make projects look expensive and store-bought. Terrified that your project will look homemade (and not in a good way)? Add leather, and you'll be well on your way to creating something that looks and feels well designed. I like to experiment with leather strapping (old belts are useful here), leather pieces, and even leather salvaged from secondhand furniture.

## Wood

Want to add an expensive, store-bought touch to your project? Consider using wood. Planks, plywood, wood sheeting, and wooden stumps are all great for DIY projects, and even the simplest project is impressive when rendered in wood. Most hardware stores have a lumber department where they'll cut wood planks and plywood for you. I take advantage of this so I can skip the arduous task of sawing wood at home.

## Chair and table legs

It might seem like a strange addition to your toolkit, but you'll be amazed at how many projects you can create using simple chair and table legs. My first foray into furniture making was after I bought some hairpin legs, and I've never looked back. As long as you choose legs of the right length, you can transform any flat piece of wood or stone into a table, chair, bench, or planter. There are a few types of legs you might want to consider adding to your toolkit or snapping up if you ever see them for sale.

* **Hairpin:** These metal legs are on the top of my list for making furniture. They're incredibly easy to use and create a minimalist look that complements most decor styles. You can also buy hairpin legs in a colored, powder-coated finish.
* **Tapered:** These wooden legs give a mid-century feel. They look best when attached with a bracket that positions the legs at an angle. Keep your eye out for these at antique or secondhand stores. My favorites are those with brass bases.
* **Column legs:** If you're after a more modern and sleek design, a simple column leg is incredibly easy to attach and gives a minimalist look.

# Sourcing Sustainable Materials

I grew up in a sustainability-minded family, and everything we did in the house was geared toward having a smaller footprint, reducing consumption, and reducing waste. This mind-set formed the basis for my love of making and reworking what I had. And it's for this reason that I love DIY. Not only does it give you the ability to indulge your inner maker and aesthete, it also allows you to be selective about materials and opt for the most sustainable. Perfecting your space doesn't need to be to the detriment of our planet and the future of our children.

All my projects focus on adaptive reuse of materials, using materials that will last, and making projects that can be changed and adapted over time. There are a few ways that you can consider sustainable materials in your process.

## Use what you have

A great place to start sourcing items for any project is in your own home, as you may find you have unused materials, furniture, or tools that can be repurposed or revitalized into a new project. And trust me, it feels great to be able to breathe new life into something that's been gathering dust in your home!

*Reuse + recycle*

It doesn't have
to be new to
be great!

## Use secondhand items

Need more tools or materials? Start by looking for secondhand items—you'll often find what you need being thrown away by someone else.

* **Online forums:** Increasingly, online forums such as Pay it Forward are filled with secondhand items that can be either repurposed or pulled apart into their usable components.
* **Secondhand stores:** Antiques stores and secondhand stores are overflowing with materials you can use for your projects. By sourcing secondhand materials, you're increasing the life spans of those items, making your project low-impact and pretty much guilt-free!
* **Junk shops:** It might seem crazy, but my favorite activity is visiting my local junk shop. It's a store attached to the local garbage dump, filled with items that have been saved from landfill. If you have a project in mind, whether it's a table or a wall hanging, this is a great place to hunt for what you need.

## Use materials that will last

The hardware store is one place that I could spend hours, if not days. And buying new items for your projects is often essential, particularly when it comes to tools. When shopping for new materials, I like to think about choosing those that will last and don't cost the earth to make.

# Ask Geneva

## HOW DO I DESIGN A SPACE THAT MY PARTNER WILL LIKE AS MUCH AS I DO?

**Q** I love decorating, but it's difficult to find a balance between what my boyfriend likes and the way I want to decorate the house. How do we meet in the middle and still feel like the house is unique to each of us?

**A** Whether it's your partner or a roommate, it can be hard to meet the needs and wants of everyone under the same roof. Some people are happy with whatever you like, but if your partner has more rigid views, here are a few ways to decorate so that you'll both love your home.

### Create a mood board together

It's easy to have a blanket rule about things like furniture, colors, and art, but often it's useful to see these things in context. Colors and shapes can be used to balance out a space so that it suits everyone, and this is something you're more likely to be able to understand if you look at some images together.

### Have a neutral base

Go for neutral tones as a base for your space, which will make it flexible and adaptable. For bigger furniture pieces, opt for lighter, neutral colors in cool tones that can be brought to life with the help of other items and accessories.

### Find the colors that work for you

When it comes to designing a space, color choice can be the most polarizing decision. I'm lucky that Ben doesn't mind a little bit of pink (or a lot!), but I know others, particularly men, don't feel the same. It's best to find some common ground on color, which might mean letting go of some stronger shades like pink or red and using softer shades like green or blue.

### Take a room

Don't feel bad if it's easier to go neutral in much of the house and then have key rooms for yourselves that you decorate. Split it up so that everyone feels like they have a space to call their own.

### Make decisions together

As fun as it might seem to buy a rattan princess chair on a whim and then figure out the rest later, this isn't the best way to create a space that you'll both enjoy. It might become the rattan elephant in the room! Make the big decisions together.

### Be prepared to compromise

You have to be willing to give a little and take a little. At the end of the day, it's unlikely that you'll be able to decorate the space with everything you want, and the same is true of your partner. But don't be afraid to haggle for the things that you do really want!

I'm lucky that Ben is openminded about colors—in fact, he suggested this pink and raw wood door!

# Reversible Ways to Update Your Rental Space

There's a lot to be said for the flexibility of renting— you can move every now and again, you can pack it all up and go traveling, and . . . no mortgage! But when it comes to decorating, renting can present a bit of a challenge, with bathroom renovations, kitchen upgrades, and other major changes pretty much out of the question. In case you're looking at your rented space and thinking, "I wish I could knock down that wall," never fear—there are plenty of ways to update and personalize your space without getting structural. And even if you do live in your own home, these little tweaks are useful as a means of updating your space on a tight budget.

First of all, it's very important that you check what your lease says and/or what your landlord's policy is regarding what you're permitted to do in your space. Some will be more relaxed than others, but don't be surprised if you're required to leave the property in its original condition when you move out.

## Textiles

Textiles are the easiest little tweak in the book. They give a space so much personality without requiring drastic changes. I recommend starting with a rug. Although rugs are often on the expensive side, they'll make the biggest improvement to your space, particularly if you're dealing with some not-so-nice flooring or ugly carpet. A nice big jute rug is a great way to create a minimalist and modern feel; choose one that goes from wall to wall for a new-carpet look without the cost or hassle. Next, choose some smaller textiles like cushions, throws, and curtains to top off your color or decor scheme. Updated curtains can also completely transform a space.

## Lighting

You're probably not going to want to hire an electrician to change the lighting in a rental, so you're going to have to work with what you've got. However, there are plenty of options for personalizing the lighting. Use oversized pendant lights and lampshades to add a feature to a room. If you're dealing with poorly placed lights or bad bulbs, add some lamps to give the space a warm feel.

## Shelves

Shelves are the perfect way to create a space that feels uniquely yours, and there are lots of options for integrating shelves into rental spaces. Floating shelves are lovely, but you may not be allowed to mess with the walls. If you *are* allowed to add the odd nail (ask first!), hanging leather shelves have less impact on the wall than floating shelves, since they require only two small nails. Otherwise, use shelves that stand on the floor, like simple rectangular shelving or shelves made from a ladder.

## Plants

To me, a house isn't a home without indoor plants. And if your rental doesn't have outdoor space, you're going to want to bring the outdoors in. Hanging plants, big feature potted plants, and smaller plants all add interest to your home without jeopardizing your lease. They also do a great job of disguising ugly walls and floors.

## Baskets

Baskets are another decor item that adds texture to your space without too much color or distraction. They're great for storage, making them functional as well as pretty. Baskets are perfect in spaces like the kitchen and laundry room that require lots of different ways to store (aka cover up) items like food supplies and clothing, and they also make great planters.

*Prop it up!*

## Art

Art is often the cherry on top when it comes to interior design, and even one or two inexpensive pieces can breathe life and uniqueness into a space. It can be a challenge to hang art in a rental space if you aren't permitted to nail anything into the walls, but there are lots of options for displaying your art: place it on top of a cabinet or on a shelf, or lean larger pieces against a wall. There are also other options for hanging it—for lighter pieces, use 3M Command hooks that don't leave a mark, or use Blu Tack to hang posters.

## Mirrors

I've often found that rental homes could benefit from removing a wall to really open up a space, but that's not likely to happen. One way to open up rooms without the huge expense of demolition is to lean some big mirrors against the walls. They don't need to be expensive. Look for large ones that really feel as if you've inserted a door in the wall.

## A few other ideas . . .

If you're looking to take the upgrades a little bit further, painting is a great way to make a big change without knocking out a wall. Simply ask your landlord what they think, and know that often you'll have to revert the space to its original condition when you leave. Wall decals can be used to create the same effect. Another idea is to swap the knobs and hardware in the kitchen and bathroom.

Even in
the most basic
secondhand store
you're likely to
find a little
home update.

# The Best Secondhand Items for Styling Your Space

I talk a lot about designing a space that feels real, lived in, and not like a showroom. But how do you actually achieve that? For me, it means adding different items and mixing up the decor so it feels layered rather than static. And that's where buying secondhand comes in! I absolutely love the depth that's created by adding antiques or secondhand pieces to a space. It's the perfectly imperfect nature of these items that gives your space life. You don't need to buy a big piece of furniture to get this effect—a few small items here and there won't cost a lot, but they can add so much interest and character to your space. And the best part? Buying secondhand is eco-friendly.

## Books

I have a fascination with unusual books from second-hand stores—the stranger, the better. I love old book covers and colorful hardcover books, for reading as well as the depth they bring to a space. Keep your eye out for pretty covers that you can match to the decor and colors in a room.

## Mirrors

Take even a cursory look around an antiques store and you'll find mirrors of all shapes and sizes, and it's this variety that adds serious personality to your space. In the last few years I've found round mirrors, arched mirrors, antiques with decorative edges, and so many more. They don't cost too much and make such a big difference.

## Baskets

Investing in older baskets bought from an antiques store is a great way to add depth to your space and give it more personality.

## Artwork

I have yet to fully embrace buying original artwork. I have to admit that most of the pieces I like are outside my price range. But that doesn't mean I have to opt for cheap knockoff prints or dull still-life pictures. Flea markets are great places to find artwork that has a life and a history.

## Ceramics

You'll always find me hunting through the ceramics section, no matter how boring and bland the second-hand store. It really pays to keep your eyes open. No matter where I am, I always manage to find amazing secondhand terracotta vases, retro cups and milk jugs, and handmade mugs.

## Lamps

Lamps are an opportunity to experiment with detail and style. And, in this case, go vintage or go home! I love everything about a fringed retro lamp, an '80s-inspired ceramic shell lamp, or anything with a pleated paper shade. Consider swapping out old or ugly shades if the base is good.

A bedroom refresh is as easy as swapping a rug and adding some decor items from other rooms.

# Ask Geneva

## HOW CAN I REDECORATE MY SPACE WITHOUT SPENDING ANY MONEY?

**Q** Decorating is something that makes me so happy, but often I want to refresh my space and have exactly zero dollars to spend. How can I redecorate my space without spending any money?

**A** This is one of my favorite challenges—how to refresh a space on a tight or zero budget. Over time I've worked out that there are plenty of ways to update your space that don't cost anything at all. Read on for my tips and tricks.

### Rearrange the furniture

This really can transform a whole room. And it's easy! All you need is a little time and some muscle power. Consider whether the whole room can be reoriented or whether the main piece of furniture can swap walls. It's best to have a measuring tape on hand—there's nothing worse than moving heavy, bulky furniture only to find that it doesn't fit.

*Measure first!*

### Cull your space

When in doubt, edit. I'm a fan of a good clean out, and also of being selective about what I bring into my house in the first place. Crowding too many things into a room can make it feel small and claustrophobic, which often gives the impression that there's something wrong with the decor. Sometimes all you need to do is introduce a bit of negative space (emptiness!) to a room to make it feel as if you've had a major renovation!

### Upcycle items in your house

You'll be amazed at how many items in your home can benefit from being upcycled. Painting furniture is a really easy way to start (see page 42), and you can also give cupboards new fronts, add new knobs to drawers, or get creative and create a side table from an old piece of marble.

### Sign up for swaps

I admit that I have a major addiction to eBay and other online classified sites. Often you can find pieces that people want to get rid of, and all they cost are your time to go and pick them up. Chances are these sorts of items will need a little TLC, but it's worth it. And don't discount garage sales where items are practically free, especially at the end of the day.

# Painting Furniture

I know it can be controversial, but I absolutely love painting wooden furniture. Some people feel that it should be practically illegal to paint wood, but to that I say: you only live once! Personally, I think painting furniture allows you to inject personality into a space without going to the trouble of painting a whole wall or choosing colored tiles. It's a technique we've used a lot in our renovation, and it's also an instant update for an old piece of furniture. Of course, if you have a very expensive piece of wooden furniture, it's probably best not to cover it in paint. Instead, choose some inexpensive pieces that, ideally, aren't in the best shape and would be improved by a coat of paint.

## STEP 1. PREPARATION

To avoid any unwanted paint marks in your working space, place your furniture on a tarp or painter's drape. It always helps to have some damp rags handy when you're painting to wipe up spills or splashes.

## STEP 2. CLEANING

Prepping is an important part of the painting process to ensure a smooth, even, and lasting finish. Begin by wiping any dust off the surface of the furniture. You might want to wash it if it's particularly dirty.

## STEP 3. SANDING

Next, it's a good idea to sand the furniture, especially if it already has a layer of paint over the wood. Start with a coarse-grain sandpaper, then move to a finer grain for the final sanding. Sand all of the surfaces to remove as much old paint as possible.

## STEP 4. APPLY PRIMER

Following the direction of the wood grain, apply a white primer. This is particularly important if the paint color you've chosen is lighter than the existing color or base color. Allow the primer to dry, ideally overnight.

## STEP 5. RE-SAND

Once the primer has dried, give your furniture another rub down with some fine-grain sandpaper so that the surface is very smooth.

## STEP 6. APPLY PAINT

Apply the first coat of paint. Allow it to dry completely before adding a second coat. You may need to apply two or three coats of paint for an even finish. Exterior, oil-based paints work well for furniture that will get a lot of wear; otherwise, you can use a simple wall paint. Use a small paintbrush for chairs and items with lots of crevices, and a bigger paintbrush or roller for tables and other large pieces of furniture.

## STEP 7. APPLY GLOSS

Consider how the furniture will be used and whether it needs an extra protective layer. If desired, apply a layer of gloss paint. If you prefer a matte finish, you can skip this step.

# Indoor Plants

I'm a huge indoor plant enthusiast. There's not one room where I wouldn't suggest adding some plants. Not only are they great for air quality, they help to bring life to a space—literally!

Luckily, you don't have to have the greenest of thumbs to keep plants around the house. However, before you go buy a forest of plants from your local nursery, it's worth considering the time and energy you'll be able to put into caring for your plants. Depending on the species, some will require a little more TLC, while others are known to be virtually unkillable. Here are some tips for caring for your indoor plants.

## Sunlight

All plants need sunlight to photosynthesize, but the type of sunlight needed by each plant differs. Some plants like direct sun rays hitting their leaves, while others prefer reflected sunlight. It may be a case of trial and error to find out if your plant is receiving the correct amount of light. You'll be able to tell if your plant is exposed to too much light if the leaves are dull and have brown edges or spots.

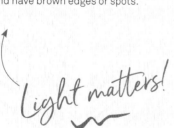

*Light matters!*

## Watering and drainage

The way you water your indoor plants will largely determine their longevity, as incorrect watering is the main cause of death. In general, some plants like their roots constantly moist (but not wet), while others prefer a couple of inches or so of their soil to dry out between waterings. Providing sufficient drainage prevents plants from drowning or developing root rot from sitting in wet soil. A good indicator of when your plant needs watering is to touch the surface of the soil or poke your finger into it to see whether it's moist or dry. Knowing if your plants are receiving the right amount of water comes down to observation, practice, and experimentation, because each plant will react differently depending on its location and size. You'll notice that you need to water more frequently in warmer months than in colder months. Refer to the plant-by-plant guide on pages 46 and 47 for more details about watering.

## Cleaning

It's important to clean indoor plants often to rid them of dust and insects, and to prevent disease. Dust and grime isn't just an aesthetic issue—it actually blocks the pores on the plant's leaves, impairing its ability to breathe. For smaller plants, use a clean, damp cloth to wipe the leaves. Give larger plants a rinse in the shower or sink.

Check the plant label or ask the nursery staff which plants are best for your conditions.

**ZANZIBAR GEM**

**SNAKE PLANT**

**POTHOS**

# My Favorite Easy-to-Grow Indoor Plants

## Zanzibar Gem

This is one of my favorite plants. Given half a chance, it will flourish in pretty much any space. The rich green hue of the leaves is the perfect complement to most decor schemes. It handles low lighting well and should be kept away from direct sunlight. It's a tough plant when it comes to watering and likes to be kept on the dry side; you can even let the soil become dusty. It's best to give the plant a thorough watering bi-monthly, but make sure you don't allow it to sit in water afterward, because this will cause root rot and the leaves will turn yellow.

## Snake Plant

Also known as mother-in-law's tongue, this plant is a great indoor plant for beginners because it flourishes in any lighting condition from bright indirect sunlight to shade. It can go for up to a month without water, so make sure you keep the soil relatively dry; it's better to underwater than overwater. I give my snake plant a quarter of a cup of water every few weeks, making sure the soil has dried out between each watering. If the leaves are drooping and becoming slimy, it means that the soil is too wet, so remove any affected leaves and adjust your watering frequency. Occasionally, it may be necessary to prune the leaves, because the point of the leaf can be very sharp. Simply clip off the points whenever they appear.

## Pothos

This plant thrives on neglect and can grow under basically any conditions. It prefers moderate to low lighting conditions, even artificial office lights. The pothos flourishes with sporadic watering, making it very easy to grow. However, as with the snake plant, don't allow the soil to become swampy, as the pothos is susceptible to root rot. Check to see that the top 2 in (5 cm) of soil has dried out before watering. Each plant is different, but if you notice that your pothos is wilted, yellow, or spotted and doesn't have much new growth, you'll need to review your watering habits. The best features of this plant? It can grow in soil or in a vase of water, with its trailing vines reaching up to 8 feet (2.5 meters), and I've found it to be virtually unkillable!

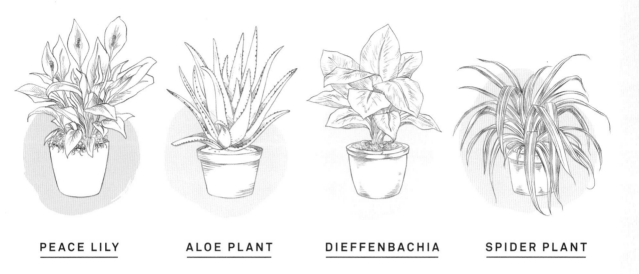

**PEACE LILY**          **ALOE PLANT**          **DIEFFENBACHIA**          **SPIDER PLANT**

## Peace Lily

Peace lilies, with their distinctive white flowers and dark, glossy leaves, can usually tolerate low lighting, making them perfect for bathrooms and dark corners. If the leaves are turning yellow, it means the plant is receiving too much light. If the leaves turn brown or have brown streaks, the plant has been burned from direct sunlight. Peace lilies typically require watering at least once a week, and they like the soil to be kept moist. Note that they are potentially toxic to humans and animals, so keep them out of reach of children and your furry friends.

## Aloe Plant

Believe it or not, aloe isn't just a sunburn soother. I love the dark leaves, and it makes a lovely addition to lots of different rooms in the house. Place aloe in a sunny spot, otherwise it will become dormant. Water the plant once every two weeks, and wait until the soil dries out before watering again—keeping the soil moist will cause the roots to rot. Limp or brown leaves also signal overwatering.

## Dieffenbachia

Dieffenbachia is an easy plant to grow and adds a lush, tropical look to a room. It grows best in bright, indirect light. While it can tolerate low light, note that its growth will slow dramatically. Once given more light, it will quickly begin to grow again. Dieffenbachia grows best in dry soil. Don't water the plant until the top 2 in (5 cm) of soil is dry, then water thoroughly at the base of the plant. If the leaves droop, it's usually a sign that the plant needs to be watered.

## Spider Plant

The spider plant gets its name from the spiderlike offshoots, or spiderettes, that hang from the mother plant, resembling spiders on a web. It's known as one of the most versatile indoor plants and is one of the easiest to grow. Spider plants are suitable for a wide range of conditions, and they don't suffer from many problems, apart from brown leaf tips.

# Easy Planter Ideas (That Don't Involve Repotting!)

Full disclosure: maintaining and looking after plants can be a lot of work—from watering to finding the right spot to figuring out what's going on when they suddenly wilt. Repotting is another task that I have to admit to not liking at all; it manages to rain on all my plant-buying parades. But pots are so key to the overall aesthetics of your plant, and short of buying plants that are already in pots (very expensive!), you're going to want to swap out that plastic brown one you get from the nursery. But sometimes you just don't have time for repotting, which is where a few creative planters come in. Admittedly, most of these are temporary options and aren't suitable for long-term use, but they're ideal if you want to put off repotting.

## The fabric wrap

Got a spare tea towel or piece of fabric lying around the house? Simply fold it in half or thirds so it's the width of the pot, then wrap it around the pot, using a safety pin or two to secure it in place.

## The basket

It will come as no surprise that I'm suggesting using a basket. Sometimes I even prefer a basket to a new pot! Just remember to put the tray of your plant pot into the bottom of the basket so you don't ruin the basket when you water your plant.

## The dust bag

Have you noticed that dust bags have become a major part of the packaging for many items you buy online? Handbags, swimwear, jewelry—so many items now arrive in a dust bag. It makes sense, because they're lighter than boxes, less expensive to ship, and more sustainable. The best part is that they can be reused. It does mean that you can be inundated with dust bags, but luckily they make fantastic plant bags!

*Reuse + recycle*

Tea towels make great plant wraps!

# A Guide to Rugs

I've had a decade-long obsession with rugs and the way they improve and basically make a room. Even a cheap rug can tie a whole room together. Rugs are also great for making a room feel more cozy, and they can improve acoustics by providing soft surfaces in a room with hard floors. And don't think rugs are only suitable for covering hard floors—they can also add style to a carpeted space and cover up an unsightly carpet! There are some rules to follow when choosing a rug. It all comes down to room size, rug placement, and what else is going on in the space. It pays to learn as much as you can before making the leap.

## Persian rugs

Persian rugs are a type of oriental rug made in Iran using a single looping knot. They're the leaders in oriental rugs, from the stately Sultanabad carpets to the geometric and abstract tribal carpets of Heriz. They're most commonly made of wool, although they can also be made of silk, which is extremely precious and long-lasting. Combined with the low pile of their weave, Persian rugs are durable and strong, making the vintage rug variety highly sought after.

## Turkish rugs

Traditional Turkish rugs (or carpets) are similar in appearance to Persian rugs, although constructed differently. They're handmade by artisans using a double loop knot. Made from fibers such as wool and silk, Turkish rugs are woven with a low pile in a wide array of styles determined by the Turkish city in which they originated. Turkish rugs were originally used as flooring in nomadic tents, so they're strong, durable, and a great temperature controller in a living space.

## Kilim rugs

Kilims are flat-woven tapestry rugs originally from Turkey, but the term *kilim* can also refer to similarly woven rugs from Scandinavia, Persia, and Morocco, each with their own distinct designs. Kilims are most commonly made of wool, although they're also made from hemp and cotton fibers. They can be woven in a wide range of motifs, making them a popular choice to add pattern and color to a space. However, because of the nature of the flat weave, kilims are much less durable than rugs with a pile, which gives protection to the flat-woven base.

## Beni Ourain rugs

Beni Ourains are Moroccan rugs that are made from wool, with a high, thick pile. They're dichromatic, usually white with bold, black geometric patterns. The neutral colors of these rugs make them popular for large, bright, minimalist interiors. However, the light base color makes dirt and scuff marks easily visible, so it's best to avoid placing a Beni Ourain rug in areas of high traffic or in homes with pets or children.

## Boucherouite rugs

Boucherouite rugs are hand-loomed by village women in remote Moroccan Berber tribes. They're often made out of clothing fabric scraps, which gives them a tufted feel, and they typically contain many bright colors. Highly textured, hooked rag rugs like these can look beautiful, but they're tricky to clean, so they aren't the best choice for high-traffic areas or if you have pets or children.

## Natural rugs

As the name suggests, these rugs are made out of strong plant fibers such as jute, sisal, seagrass, bamboo, or coir. They're flat-woven, but, unlike kilims, rugs that are produced from these natural fibers are extremely durable and versatile, making them ideal for high-traffic areas. These hardy, contemporary rugs are a great alternative to rugs made out of wool or cotton and can bring a casual look and feel to a room.

## Size and placement

### In the living room . . .

Ideally, the rug should be large enough to fit all of your living room furniture on it, as this will help pull the room together. Alternatively, if your rug isn't big enough to include all of the furniture, placing the front legs of each piece on the rug creates a good balance. It's best to avoid a rug that's too small and floats in the middle of the space. If you have a rectangular layout, go for a rectangular rug, not a round one.

DO

DON'T

### In the dining room . . .

If you can, make sure that all the legs of the chairs are inside the rug edges, with a good amount of rug bordering the setup. In most cases, rugs that are smaller than your furniture feel a bit awkward. They also make it hard to move the dining chairs in and out from the table, so if in doubt, go for a bigger rug. For a more styled look, match the shape of the tabletop to your rug shape.

DO
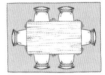 

DON'T
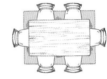 

### In the bedroom . . .

The best layout for the bedroom is using a large rug to frame the bed and bedside tables, as this makes the room feel bigger. If you can't find a rug large enough, placing a runner on either side of the bed works well by adding some symmetry. Another option is having the two back legs of the bed off the rug. Note that the thicker your rug, the more height difference there will be between the two ends.

DO

DON'T

A long-lasting rug is a great option for a kitchen, as it helps to soften a hard space.

*Tip*

Don't be afraid
to ask the store
if you can take
the rug home to
check how it
looks. Many
stores will let
you return or
exchange it if
it's not right.

# Tips for Buying Rugs

## Budget

When it comes to setting a budget for your rug, affordability is obviously relative—rugs tend to be expensive due to the work that goes into making them, particularly the larger ones. But there are plenty of cheaper options out there. A little tip from me: lots of rug shops are beautifully curated, making it easy to imagine the rugs in your home, but if you want a good-quality rug at a bargain price, it's worth trawling the stores that sell directly from Turkey, Pakistan, and Morocco. The styling might not be as pretty, but the rugs are often just the same, usually with a smaller markup.

## Shipping

If you're buying a rug online, look at the shipping cost—because rugs are often very heavy, the shipping can sometimes cost almost as much as the rug itself. Look for sellers that offer free shipping, but be aware that the shipping cost is often rolled into the item price, so it's worth comparing. And keep an eye out for "free shipping" promotions that some stores will offer from time to time. This is when you can save some cash!

## Size

Before purchasing your rug, make sure you measure the size of your room and the size of the area your furniture occupies, so you know the proportions of the space you're working with. Depending on the country of origin of the online store, standard rug sizes are usually given in feet (although sometimes they aren't specified), so "5 × 7" indicates a rug that's 150 × 210 cm.

## Rug terminology

Rugs have a language all their own, so it's useful to understand the terminology before you buy.

* **Yarn:** This is the strand of fibers used in creating the rug.
* **Pile:** This is yarn that's looped to a flat-woven base and stands upright, giving the rug a fluffy look and feel. Pile can be looped, cut, high, or low. It's also good to note that although the price of rugs will vary greatly depending on the size, generally speaking, rugs with pile weaves and oriental or vintage origins will be more costly than their flat-woven, commercially produced cousins.
* **Overdyed:** This is a technique that's traditionally performed on vintage handwoven wool carpets. Creating this look involves bleaching, dyeing, and washing the old carpets, which produces a rug that's richly saturated in color yet you can still see the original pattern peeking through.
* **Knotted:** This is usually a high-quality handmade woven rug that's created by tying each yarn tuft to the warp strand. Knot count refers to the number of knots per square inch.
* **Flat-woven:** Rugs with the yarn woven through and along the warps.
* **Antique:** If the quality is good, an older rug is generally more valuable than a newer one due to the way rugs have historically been produced. Antique is often not easy to define—sometimes it refers to more than fifty years in age, and at other times it means more than a hundred years old. Unless you specifically want an antique rug, I think the most important thing to understand is whether a rug has been handmade or commercially made, as this will make the biggest difference in quality.

# The Entryway

*Make it welcoming*

# Welcome home

Older, bigger houses had a designated hallway, but many don't have that anymore. You might step straight through the front door into your living room. Whatever your setup, the entryway is the first place you experience when you come into your home. It's where you hang up your coat and sort through a pile of mail or a mountain of shopping. It's also the last space you pass through on your way out the door as you grab your coat, keys, or bag. The entryway is a surprisingly important part of the home, but it also has the potential to become a very cluttered space.

We all want to be able to leave the house in the morning with a positive mind-set and come home to a happy space. And, while you might not realize it, a disorganized, unwelcoming entryway can alter your mood when you walk through the door. It's worth putting some thought into how it looks and functions, to create a space that's easy to keep organized and stylish at the same time. In this chapter, I'll outline what you need to include in this area, and show you how easy it is to DIY it into a welcoming space.

It's worth putting some thought into your entryway, to create a space that's easy to keep organized and stylish at the same time.

# Checklist for a Welcoming Entryway

Chances are, whether you've designed it this way or not, there's a part of your home (most likely near the door) that functions as an entryway. You probably dump things there as you walk in, and chances are it could be better organized and look much nicer. The key to creating a space that works is all about making sure it has a number of different functional elements. What you include will obviously depend on the amount of space available, but even if you have a very small space, a little bit of thought, some smart storage, and a few other design considerations can make it much more user-friendly. It might even change your life!

## ☐ Seating

Providing seating in your entryway is ideal for creating a transitional space where shoes and other items can be removed easily. Finding the right type of seating is key to creating a space that is not only organized but comfortable and inviting as well. I find that benches are really versatile and perfect for sitting on, and they can also act as storage for items that are brought into and taken out of the house.

## ☐ Storage

Storage that helps organize (and hide) essentials and clutter is ideal in any entryway. A cabinet, shelves, baskets, or boxes all act as ideal places for your shoes, bags, and other items that need to be stored. Obviously, the amount of storage you can include will depend on the space itself, but even a couple of matching baskets placed underneath a bench will be helpful in organizing a stylish and functional space.

## ☐ Hanging space

One of the easiest ways to create an efficient space is by using the walls for organization. Installing wall hooks is a great option, especially in small spaces or corridors where you want to reduce the amount of clutter (like coats, bags, and umbrellas) on the floor.

## ☐ A catch-all tray

"Have a place for everything" is useful advice for all of us. The best place to start? The entryway! Having a few trays that provide a home for keys, your purse, and other small items can really help to organize you as you leave the house, meaning less chance of forgetting essential items or trying to find them at the last minute . . . and a better start to the day.

### 🪟 A mirror

If there's one thing that makes your exit smooth and speedy, it's being able to do a quick check of your hair and makeup before you run out the door. Hanging a mirror in your entryway will save you precious time each and every day.

### 🪟 A rug

A rug is a great way to add personality to any space, and that goes for entryways, too. Keep in mind that this transitional space experiences lots of coming and going, so you're going to need a rug that's durable and not too fragile. I like to use jute and other tough materials that stand up to constant traffic and are easily able to be cleaned.

### 🪟 A touch of style

Once you have all the basics in place, it's time to add some pieces just for aesthetics—like plants, cushions, and art. Try to keep it simple, though—you don't want your entryway to be so cluttered that it becomes hard to use.

# Rug-Covered Bench

*Project*

This bench seat is a beautiful blend of style and function. I fell in love with the simplicity of using hairpin legs and wood to create benches years ago. Here, I've used a rug as upholstery to make a piece with a serious amount of personality. Another great thing about this project is that it injects style into your space through the use of textiles, without having to add cushions or other decor elements that might clutter your entryway. This versatile project will last for years. You can even re-cover the bench in the longer term.

## HOW TO

**1**

Cut the plywood to size or ask the hardware store to cut it for you.

**2**

Cut the foam cushion to fit your plywood or ask the foam store to cut it for you. It's best if the foam is about ¾ in (2 cm) smaller on all sides. This helps the rug fit over the foam and plywood.

**3**

Cut the foam batting so that it's large enough to cover the foam cushion and plywood and be stapled underneath.

**4**

Place the rug upside down and arrange the batting, foam cushion, and plywood on top. Use a staple gun to staple the rug to the plywood. It's best to really take your time and plan out the corners, and make sure the rug and top design are going to fit your bench.

**5**

Finally, drill pilot holes into the underside of the bench to attach the legs, then screw the legs in place.

STEP 4

STEP 5

## YOU NEED

* Plywood sheet or plank: 10 x 35½ in (25 x 90 cm)
* A rug large enough to cover the batting and foam
* Foam cushion * Foam batting * 4 hairpin legs
* Power drill * 8 screws * Sharp scissors or a
craft knife * Basic toolbox (page 30)

*Tip*

This bench
is perfect for
renters who want
to create an
entryway space
without damaging
the walls or
building anything
significant.
Of course, it will
also go with you
when you leave!

READER'S DIGEST ATLAS OF AUSTRALIA

Hooks are an ideal way to provide storage that doesn't take up very much space.

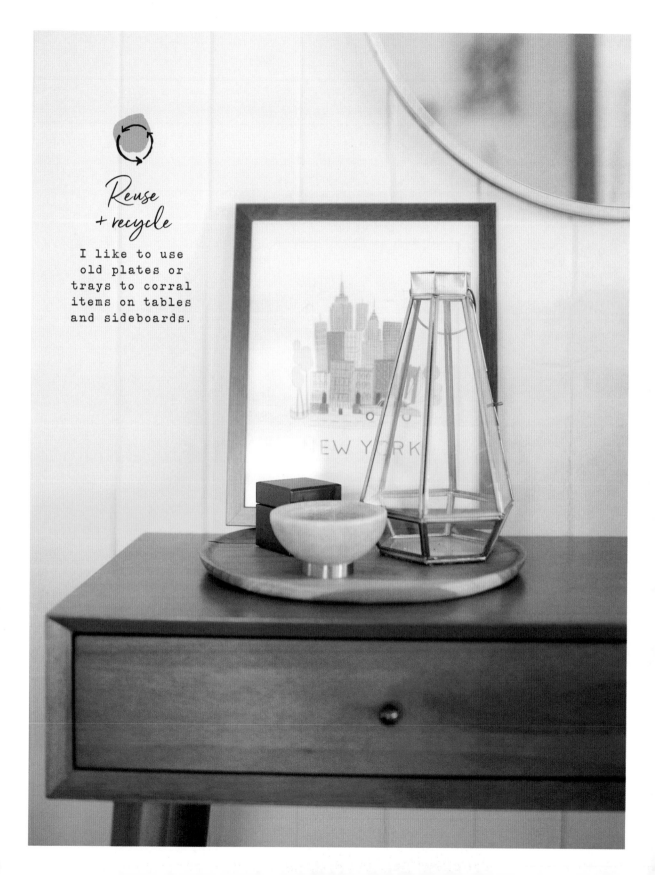

## Reuse
## + recycle

I like to use
old plates or
trays to corral
items on tables
and sideboards.

## Tip

Looking to choose a plant for your entryway? Opt for plants that grow vertically rather than horizontally, so that they take up less space while providing green relief. A snake plant (see page 46) is a great option.

# Mid-Century Plant Stand

*Project*

Plants and entryways are a perfect combination, because it's lovely to be welcomed home by some greenery. A plant stand is always a good idea, as it lifts the plant off the ground and frees up space on the floor for your shoes and storage baskets. This project is fairly simple as far as furniture building is concerned and doesn't require any previous woodworking knowledge. And by using a sturdy cutting board rather than having to cut the wood, I've made it seriously easy. I chose to paint the cutting board, but you can leave the wood finish if you prefer.

STEP 1

STEP 2

## HOW TO

**1**

Measure and mark 10 in (25 cm) from the bottom of your dowels.

**2**

Lay a bracket on each dowel so that it lines up with the marking, with the hole centered. Mark the holes, then drill pilot holes and screw the brackets onto the dowels.

**3**

Turn the cutting board upside down and use a ruler to draw two lines through the center that intersect at right angles.

**4**

Take one of the dowels and line up the bracket so that one of the marked lines on the board shows through the hole in the bracket. Make a mark for the pilot hole, then repeat for the other three dowels. Drill the four pilot holes.

**5**

Attach the legs by screwing the brackets onto the base of the cutting board.

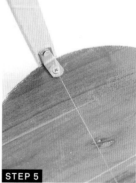

STEP 5

## YOU NEED

* A cutting board or precut circle of wood
* 4 square dowels * 4 x ½ in (1 cm) wide L-brackets * 8 screws * Power drill
* Basic toolbox (page 30)

## Ask Geneva

## HOW DO I STYLE A TINY ENTRYWAY OR HALLWAY?

**Q** I love the idea of having a beautiful entryway to help organize my life, but I have zero space for it. How can I create a small entryway?

**A** Up until a few years ago I had very little concept of what an entryway was, and mistakenly thought that I needed a big house with a hall foyer or giant mudroom to get the benefits of an entryway. But over time I've come to understand that you can create a functional entryway regardless of how large your space is. You could even argue that the smaller your space is, the more you need an organized (and stylish!) entry area. Here are a few tips for creating an entryway when you don't have much space.

### Mark out the space
Find a blank wall near the front door that can act as a quasi-entryway. Try to find an area that is at least 3 feet (1 meter) wide, although a small corner will also suffice.

### Use slimline furniture
A console is a great option for any entryway, but often in smaller spaces they aren't practical. Opt for a slimline bench or table instead—you can even make your own using some hairpin legs (see page 64).

### Go big on hooks
No space? No problem. Hanging space is your friend, so utilize the walls in a functional way as much as possible. This means getting some hanging coatracks, hooks on the walls, hanging shelves, and also perhaps a hat stand.

### Use a mirror
Add a hanging mirror to your space to reflect light and instantly make the space feel larger. It's also a courtesy to people arriving or leaving if they want to check how they look.

### Avoid clutter
Storage is useful in any entryway, but in a smaller space you need to be particularly mindful of keeping the space as uncluttered as possible. Be ruthless—only include items in the space that you need and ditch anything that isn't essential.

*Tip*

Looking for
easy wall hooks?
Mini wooden bowls
or doorknobs
fastened with
screws or
adhesive strips
are perfect!

Create a hanging
entryway with
the tutorial on
page 118, using
a dowel instead
of a branch.

*Reuse + recycle*

I love to keep
leather scraps
for projects
like these.

# Leather Key Tags

*Project*

Hand stamping is a skill that I've been experimenting with for years. Not only does it bring so much joy to stamp away on leather or brass, but these tags are ideal for integrating organization into even the smallest elements of your routine. No more rummaging around wondering if this is the key to the front door or the back door! Once you get the hang of using stamping letters, you'll want to use them to label the bottles in your kitchen, on basket tags for your bathroom, and just about everywhere else.

**STEP 4**

## HOW TO

**1**

Cut the leather to the shape you want. I chose rectangular shapes, but you could also use circles or travel-tag shapes.

**2**

Secure the leather tags to the cutting board with tape.

**3**

Carefully stamp the tags, steadying the stamp and hammer and making sure you apply even pressure.

**4**

Hammer a nail into the top of each tag to make a hole. Add the key rings.

Take a bit of time to get used to using the letter stamps before you start on the leather. You can practice on a notepad. Figure out how best to align and space the letters before using them on the leather.

## YOU NEED

\* Leather \* Metal letter stamps \* Key rings
\* Cutting board \* Basic toolbox (page 30)

# The Living Room

## Make it inviting

# Bring it to life

A living room is just that: a room in a house where we actually live. On a day-to-day basis, it's likely that the living room is one of the most well-used rooms in the house, after the kitchen. It's also likely to be a location for more formal occasions, such as hosting guests or holding parties. So the living room is a very important space to get right.

It's easy to overlook the real function of a living room as a place of gathering, relaxing, and being together and instead focus on aesthetics above all else. It's also easy to check all the function boxes but find it difficult to bring the space together in terms of its look and feel. Living rooms need to be designed as some of the most versatile and usable spaces in the home, but also styled to be welcoming and comfortable. It can be tricky! Getting the balance right in terms of how the room looks and how usable and functional it is can be a challenge, but one that's well worth tackling. In this chapter, I'll talk you through how to make and style your living room into a space where everyone will love to spend time.

Living rooms need to be designed as some of the most versatile and usable spaces in the home, but also styled to be welcoming and comfortable.

# Checklist for an Inviting Living Room

The thought of decorating a living room can be so fun and exciting that it's easy to get caught up in the cushions or textiles before you understand what's needed for the foundations of the space. Assessing how you'll use the room is key before you start figuring out the styling details. When planning a room, I always remind myself to "put the big rocks in first." I first heard this concept in relation to time management, but it applies just as much to designing a room. Start with the bigger items, then move on to the details.

## ☐ Seating

The most important question to ask about the living room is: Does it cater to your home and your family? First, think about the seating in terms of how many people you'd like to seat. You might need a sofa plus a couple of armchairs, and I like to locate a mix of chairs opposite one another so people can easily chat. It's a good idea to use the sofa as the hero piece. Because of its size, it often dictates the feel and color palette, so choose the colors and materials carefully. I prefer using neutral shades for larger pieces of furniture, adding color with textiles in cushions, rugs, and throws, which are easily updated.

## ☐ Entertainment

The living room is a fantastic space for gathering, and it's also a room in which you'll probably have a TV, a sound system, and other entertainment. It's useful to consider how these can be in the space without dominating it (see page 98).

## ☐ Tables

Choose what you need based on the size of your room. A large coffee table that caters to all the seating is great, but also consider smaller side tables if a large table won't fit or, for larger spaces, if it isn't within arm's reach of the seating.

## ☐ Lighting

Although we often think about the impact of the lighting on a room, it's also worth considering how a great lampshade or lamp makes a space look. There are few items in the house that are as functional, and also as stylish, as a lamp.

## ☐ A great rug

A big area rug will pull your living room together and make it feel comfortable and cozy. A rug also softens the space, allowing people to relax on the floor if they choose. In an open-plan living and dining space, a rug also does a great job of delineating the living space and pulling all the pieces together.

### ▢ Shelving

A bookshelf or set of low shelves is not only fantastic for storage, it also provides a space to style and share your favorite collections and inject some personality.

### ▢ Textiles

Cushions and throws are a great way to add color, personality, and warmth to a space. They also make your furniture more comfortable and inviting. I like them because they make a big statement but can also be updated easily.

### ▢ Plants

There's not one room in my house that doesn't have plants; when it comes to greenery, the more the merrier! I really love plants in the living room. Select one large plant for the corner or place a number of smaller plants on shelves or on top of the coffee table.

# Circle Hanging Planters

## *Project*

Plants add so much to any space in the house. But for me, the living room is one place that really suits the "more is more" approach to greenery. I love to plunk a big fiddle-leaf fig in the corner of the room, decorate shelves and tabletops with drapey vines, and hang plants from corners of the room that might usually be neglected. These hanging planters are a great idea for those upper reaches of the room that could do with some attention, and they're really easy to make! The materials given make three planters in different sizes.

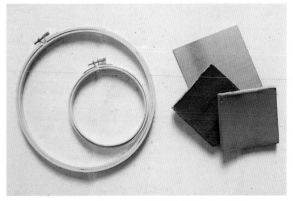

STEP 1

STEP 2

## HOW TO

**1**
For each planter, unscrew the embroidery hoops and spread them open so the space in between matches the width of the tile.

**2**
Use the glue gun to secure the top of the hoops, then glue the corners of the tile to the bottom of the hoops.

**3**
Cut about 79 in (2 m) of cord for each planter (you'll need more cord if you're hanging the planters high).

**4**
Using your glue gun, apply some glue to one end of the cord and press it onto one side of the hoop screw. Keeping the cord tight, wrap it around the hoop and screw, covering the metal and then continuing about ¾ in (2 cm) along. Secure with a dab of glue.

**5**
Measure how high you want the planter to hang, then tie a piece of cord in the center, with a loop knot at one end. Trim the cord ends.

Embroidery hoops are very versatile and can be used in lots of home decor projects. It's useful to keep a few on hand in various sizes.

## YOU NEED

* 3 embroidery hoops: 5 in (13 cm), 8½ in (22 cm), and 12 in (30 cm) * 3 square tiles: 3½ in (9 cm), 4 in (10 cm), and 4½ in (11.5 cm) * 19½ ft (6 m) of ¼ in (5 mm) cotton cord * Glue gun * Sharp scissors

## Tip

Hang your
planter from
a shelf or
from a hook
attached to
the ceiling.

No hooks!

# STYLING A LIVING ROOM

 **IT'S NOT JUST ABOUT THE TV!**

It's great to be able to kick back and watch TV in your living room, but a really great space also encourages us to read a book, chat, or take a moment to reflect on our day. The TV shouldn't be the sole focus.

 **SIMPLIFY SHELVES AND TABLETOPS**

A well-styled space doesn't need every surface covered. Overcrowding shelves, tabletops, and nooks can create a claustrophobic feel. Gather a few items together and leave the rest of the surface clear.

 **GET THE RUG SIZE RIGHT**

A great rug is essential in a living space, but the size is important. If a rug is too small, it can make a room feel off-balance or smaller than it is. See pages 51–55 for advice on choosing the right rug.

 **GET CREATIVE WITH LIGHTING**

Want to set a cozy mood in your space? The finishing touch has to be the right lighting. Although most rooms have overhead lights, low lighting that shines up onto the ceiling is a good way to make a room feel relaxing. Even a cheap floor lamp will do wonders.

 **ADD TEXTURE**

Texture helps to add contrast and interest, and make a space feel more styled and expensive. Cushions and throws are some of the cheapest ways to incorporate texture and color, and to update a space. Plants and baskets are also great options for giving life and depth.

 **WALL ART**

The living room is the place to use the walls to express your personality. A gallery wall is perfect for the living room (see pages 134–37), or a single oversized piece of art balanced on a low cupboard can pack a big punch. Don't just rely on framed pieces to add personality— hanging up rugs or tapestries works well, too.

# Leather Sling Chair

*Project*

A statement chair has the power to make a living space, but a really great chair can cost you a pretty penny. Here's a project with serious "wow" factor, without the price tag. I like to use vintage chairs, particularly ones with a classic feel that won't date, and update them with beautiful materials like leather, mud cloth, or a tufted rug. These materials are often easy to source by salvaging old pieces or looking in secondhand stores.

## HOW TO

**1**
Carefully remove the old fabric from the chair.

**2**
Cut the leather to the size of the old fabric, adding an extra 3 in (7.5 cm) of leather at each end to cover the chair rails.

**3**
Fold the leather over the top and bottom chair rails and use a staple gun to staple it in place.

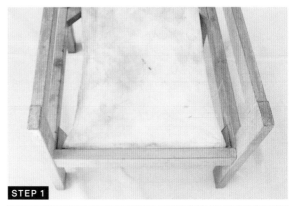
STEP 1

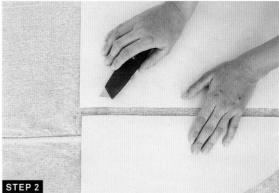
STEP 2

STEP 3

## YOU NEED

\* Upcycled armchair
\* Piece of leather to fit your chair
\* Craft knife \* Basic toolbox (page 30)

## Reuse + recycle

You can also use a sling-back beach chair for this project. Remove the dowels and fabric, then staple the leather in place before reinserting the dowels into the chair.

I think it's important
to mix new and vintage
elements in order to create an
interesting, eclectic room
that reflects who you are.

# Magnetic Art Hanger

## *Project*

Frames make a world of difference in a room—a beautiful gallery wall or framed art instantly makes a space feel more elegant and sophisticated. However, creating the mitered edges required to piece a frame together is a frustrating task that continues to confound me as an avid DIYer. Luckily, there are a few easier options, such as this magnetic art hanger. It's a simplified version of a DIY frame, perfect for hanging a simple, inexpensive piece.

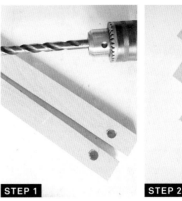

STEP 1       STEP 2

## HOW TO

**1**

Mark the placement of your magnets near the ends of the pieces of wood. Drill the markings to create indents for the magnets, making the indents deep enough for the magnets to sit flush.

**2**

Glue the magnets in place. Remember to check the polarity of the magnets so that the positive and negative sides match up for each set of wood.

**3**

Using a staple gun, staple the cord to one of the top pieces of wood (or hammer in two thumbtacks).

**4**

Insert the artwork between the wood sets.

It's important to use strong magnets for this project so they securely hold your art in place.

## YOU NEED

* 4 pieces of wood: 1 in (2.5 cm) wide by ¼ in (5 mm) thick and slightly longer than the width of your artwork
* 8 small round magnets * 16 in (40 cm) cotton cord
* Superglue * Power drill with a bit slightly larger than the magnets * Sharp scissors * Basic toolbox (page 30)

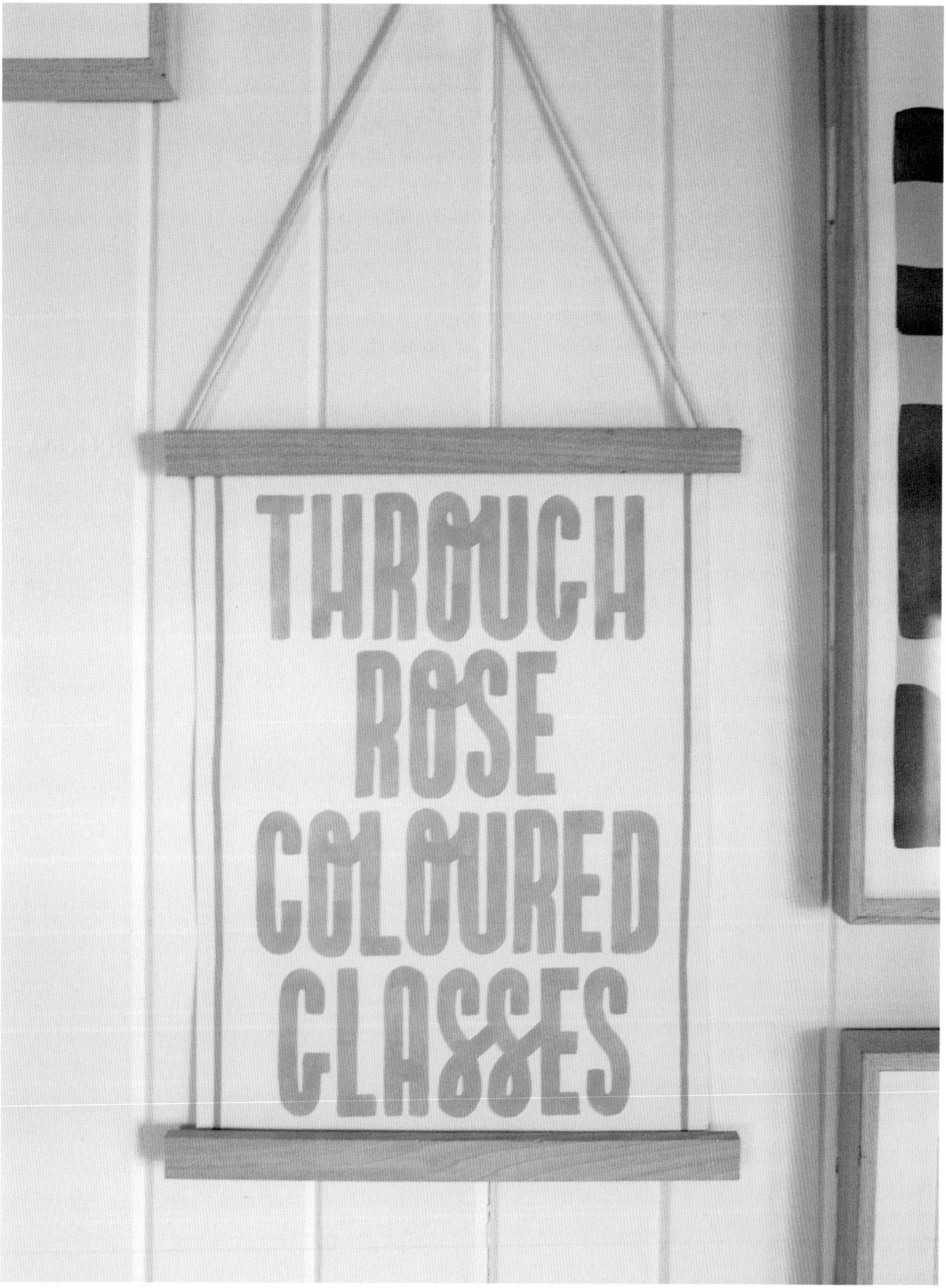
THROUGH
ROSE
COLOURED
GLASSES

Include lots of texture and a few different colors that tie into a single palette.

# STYLING SHELVES

If you thought shelves were just for storage, you'd be wrong! They're also a perfect way to display a few of your favorite things, and to bring out the color palette of your room. I like using open-fronted cupboards or floating shelves.

 **START FROM SCRATCH**

Begin with completely bare shelves—that way, you can look at them with fresh eyes, and you have a blank canvas to work with.

 **CONSIDER TONES**

For a more styled feel, consider using a tonal theme throughout your shelves. To do this, go around your house and collect items in a set color palette.

 **ANCHOR WITH LARGER ITEMS**

Start by putting all the larger items onto the shelves, such as stacks of books, vases, trays, and boxes. These items will anchor the shelves. Think about the heights that you're adding and how they fill the space.

 **ADD DETAIL AND TEXTURE**

The next step is to build on the larger items by placing smaller items on top of and around these building blocks. Think about groups and textures here.

 **TINKER WITH THE LAYOUT**

Step back to tinker and distribute the items so that they have a natural look that isn't too symmetrical. Think about materials and colors and where they're placed; arrange items with similar finishes so they aren't too close to one another.

 **ADD SOME LIFE**

As always, adding a plant or two will help to bring life and softness to the shelves. A draped hanging plant is a fantastic option.

# Reuse
## + recycle

Secondhand
stores are great
places to find
interesting
vases that will
make unique
lamps and add an
extra layer of
personality to
your space.

# Vase Lamp
## *Project*

You'll love how easy it is to turn an empty vase, jar, or bottle into a lamp that you'll use every day. Any shape will work, and I love to use quirky vases that make a statement. It can be daunting to work on anything electrical, but this project is simple to put together using a lamp kit that I bought on Etsy (see page 217). The only potentially difficult part is assembling the hardware, but there are lots of places online where you can buy lamp kits that are already assembled.

## HOW TO

### 1

Assemble the lamp kit and attach it to the vase cap that's included in the kit. I used a lamp kit with a side entry so that I didn't have to drill a hole in the ceramic vase. I just positioned the finished lamp with the cord to the back. If your lamp kit has a bottom cord entry, you'll need to drill a hole for the cord to come out.

### 2

Glue the vase cap to the top of the vase using superglue.

### 3

Once you've finished putting the lamp together, attach the lampshade to the socket fitting, then attach the light bulb.

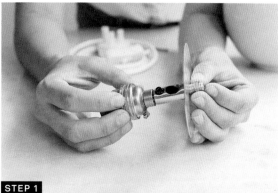

STEP 1

STEP 2

STEP 3

## YOU NEED

\* Lamp kit with side access \* Vase
\* Lampshade \* Light bulb \* Superglue

## Ask Geneva

## HOW CAN I CREATE A GORGEOUS LIVING ROOM WHEN THE TV DOMINATES THE SPACE?

Q I've loved spending time designing my living space, but one thing I don't know how to deal with is the TV. It's just so imposing, and it makes the space feel as though it has only one function—watching TV. Do you have any tips?

A One of the biggest problems with living spaces is that they're often dominated by the TV, which makes it hard to imagine doing anything in the space other than watching it. But living spaces are for so much more than that! Here are a few ideas for designing a living room around an entertainment system.

**Gallery wall**

If you plan to mount your TV on the wall, it's a great idea to create a gallery wall around the TV (see pages 134–37). This will help camouflage it and make it less of an eyesore. These days you can even buy TVs that double as artwork, displaying art on the screen when the TV is not in use.

**Box it up**

Another great option is to put your TV inside a cabinet that opens when you want to watch it, and can be closed for TV-free times. Use floor-to-ceiling cabinets or bookshelves with adjustable shelving.

**Go dark**

Paint one wall a dark color and then mount the TV on that wall. This easy camouflaging trick will mean your TV draws much less attention to itself.

**Cover it up**

If you have a wall-mounted TV, install a curtain rod above it. Then, when you want to cover the TV, you can hang a textile over it for instant art! Make sure you turn off the power first.

*Clever trick!*

Hanging textiles are a great way to disguise the TV when it's not in use!

# Magazine Shelf

Project

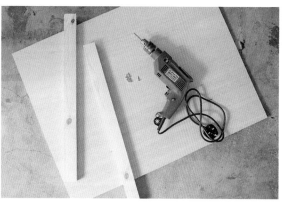

This is one of my favorite freestanding projects. It's so easy to move the shelf from one place to another—even from one room to another. And you can also swap the magazines or books on display, giving your space a fresh look. If you want to update the shelf to suit your decor, just add a stain or a fresh coat of paint. The best thing about this rack is that it's very simple to make, whether you have woodworking skills or not.

**STEP 1**

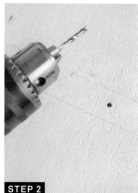
**STEP 2**

## HOW TO

### 1
Decide how far apart you want your shelves to be. I left 14 in (35 cm) between my shelves. Using a level and a square, measure and mark on the plywood where each of the shelves will go.

### 2
Drill three pilot holes through the plywood for each of the shelves to screw into—one in the center of the sheet, and two others roughly 2 in (5 cm) from either end.

### 3
Squeeze a line of wood glue along the back of the first shelf. Line it up with the markings on the plywood.

### 4
Using the pilot holes in the plywood as a guide, drill through the holes again, drilling all the way into the shelf.

### 5
Screw the wood screws through the plywood and into the shelf.

### 6
Attach the second shelf in the same way as the first.

**STEP 5**

**STEP 6**

## YOU NEED

* Plywood sheet: 31½ x 24 in (80 x 60 cm)
* 2 boards: 31½ x 2 x ¾ in (80 x 5 x 2 cm)
* Power drill * Wood glue * 6 wood screws, 1 in (2.5 cm) long * Basic toolbox (page 30)

# The Kitchen

*Make it functional + beautiful*

# *The heart of the home*

The kitchen really is the heart of the home, and it should therefore be a big focus when you're decorating. It's an important room even from a time perspective. If I were to calculate the room where I spend the most waking hours, it would have to be the kitchen. It's where we cook food for our loved ones and make memories with friends and family around the dinner table. It's the heart of the home for a reason.

Although the kitchen is sometimes seen as a purely utilitarian space, the aesthetics of your kitchen shouldn't be overlooked. Given the amount of time you spend in it, you might as well make your kitchen a place that suits your style just as much as it makes for good cooking. A great kitchen is equal parts beauty and function.

I've lived with my share of scary kitchens, from tiny corridor kitchens that had a "one in, one out" rule to giant, echoing spaces where everything I needed was a mile away. But with a few simple DIY and styling hacks, I've always been able to make the most of these rooms and turn them into spaces where I enjoyed spending time. Sometimes it might be a challenge, but trust me, it's doable!

The kitchen is where we cook food for our loved ones and make memories with friends and family around the dinner table. It's the heart of the home for a reason.

# Checklist for a Functional, Beautiful Kitchen

There are lots of ways to create a gorgeous kitchen that doesn't feel like a place where you simply slave away over a hot stove. It's important to develop a vision and then integrate functional as well as beautiful elements into the space.

### ☐ Location

Think about how you actually use your kitchen. Consider where the different activities take place and what needs to be close by to make those activities quicker and easier. Storing items close to where you use them is ideal.

### ☐ Stations

Unless your kitchen is tiny, it's useful to set up a few stations that cater to the various activities that occur in different parts of the kitchen. For example, store the items you use for making tea and coffee on a tray near the kettle, or have a caddy with olive oil, salt, and pepper near the stove. Creating stations is very simple, but they do make a difference to your daily life.

### ☐ Seating

In the past, the kitchen was more of a transitional space, but these days it's a place where people tend to gather and relax. It's essential, therefore, that there are places for people to sit. It's worth considering adding a couple of stools, a bench, or a table when you think about the layout of your kitchen.

### ☐ Storage

What's the point of a beautiful kitchen if you have nowhere to store everything you need? Having sufficient storage is essential and should be included in the form of drawers and cupboards. I love open shelving, but it only works if you have enough other storage—otherwise you risk your open shelving becoming overstuffed and messy.

## 🗒 A rug

I know that a kitchen is a controversial place to put a rug, but hear me out! A rug is the easiest way to make a space feel cozy and homey. Kitchens often suffer from feeling underdressed, and a rug is an easy way to turn that around. If you're considering putting a rug in your kitchen, it's important to find one that's suitable for the busy (and messy) kitchen space, so look for something that's durable and easy to clean.

## 🗒 A personal touch

The goal for making a home is to make it yours—a space that makes you happy to be there and shows your personality. That's why I love to add a personal touch to my kitchen, whether it be through some art, small mementos, a favorite vase, or a framed quote. I love having open shelving where I can inject some of my own style.

Tip

Have fun
experimenting
with different
types of fabric
and the amount
of time you
steep it in the
dye. Using more
avocado pits
will produce
a stronger,
deeper color.

# Avocado-Dyed Napkins

*Project*

I have long been a fan of dye and its ability to completely transform or salvage a piece of plain fabric. A few years ago, I stumbled across the idea of coloring fabrics with naturally derived dyes—from fruits, plants, and spices. I couldn't believe I had been in the dark for so long! I very quickly started experimenting with different colors and combinations. So, a word of warning: once you try natural dyeing, you might not be able to stop.

STEP 3

STEP 4

## HOW TO

**1**

Prewash and soak the fabric in warm to hot water with a gentle fabric soap. Rinse the fabric and ensure that it stays damp.

**2**

Fill a saucepan with enough water to ensure that the avocado pits and skins will be covered and the fabric will be able to move freely. Gently wash the avocado pits and skins and add them to the saucepan.

**3**

Bring to a low boil, then reduce to a simmer. Simmer until the water turns pink and then a deep maroon.

**4**

Remove the avocado skins and pits, then add the fabric. It can be immersed in the dye while the dye is simmering or after the dye has steeped and cooled. I let it simmer for 1 to 2 hours, then turn off the heat and let it steep overnight. The longer it soaks, the more vibrant the color will be.

**5**

When the fabric reaches your desired shade, remove it from the dye. Rinse it in cool to warm water with a gentle fabric soap and then hang it up to dry. Once dry, use a sewing machine to hem the fabric into napkins.

## YOU NEED

\* Linen squares \* 2 fresh avocado pits and skins per 9 oz (250 g) of fabric
\* Gentle fabric soap \* Large saucepan
\* Wooden spoon \* Sewing machine

# Ask Geneva

## HOW DO I STYLE A BEAUTIFUL KITCHEN?

**Q** The kitchen is my favorite room of the house, but I'm struggling to turn it into a gorgeous space that's in keeping with the decor in the rest of my home. How do I make my kitchen a beautiful space?

**A** We don't often think about the decor in our kitchen, and focus instead on how it functions. But no matter the actual design of your kitchen, there are lots of small tweaks you can make to ensure it's beautiful and a joy to be in—and they don't have to be costly or involve a major renovation. It's just about considering the details and putting your own personal stamp on the space.

### Clear your benchtops

A clutter-free kitchen is the first foundation of a beautifully styled space. If you're feeling like your kitchen needs a refresh, consider clearing the bench tops—find places for all of the functional, not-so-pretty items in the cupboards and start with a clean slate.

### Label it up

I have an addiction to my retro label maker. It's such a lovely detail to label all your bottles and jars, and it's also incredibly functional! Even better, by using jars instead of bags, you're taking a step toward a plastic-free and low-waste kitchen.

### Display your favorite utensils and vessels

Why put your favorite ceramics and utensils away in a cupboard or drawer when they can help style your beautiful kitchen? I like to layer wooden cutting boards by leaning them against a wall, and also display ceramic vases with wooden spoons and other nice utensils.

### Style open shelving

As long as you have enough other "hidden" storage, open shelving is such a lovely way to display some favorite kitchen items. Start by placing your favorite cookbooks on the shelves, then add some pretty ceramics and some plants.

### Display your fresh food

Fresh, seasonal produce is a feast for the tummy and also for the eyes. Use baskets to display citrus and other pretty, fresh foods. This will also make you more likely to eat them before they spoil, so it's a win-win!

In the kitchen, details like plants, cookbooks, and ceramics help create an inviting space.

# Wire Basket

*Project*

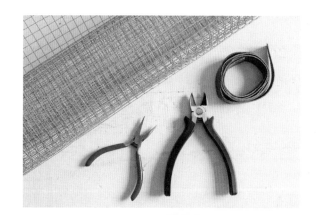

I don't think I'll ever be able to go completely minimalist, but that's understandable in the kitchen, where gadgets are essential. Storage is the love of my life, and I like to get creative when it comes to finding storage solutions that look as good as they function. If you're a sucker for kitchen gadgets, or if you just want to display your fresh market vegetables, look no further than this simple basket. Made with wire you'll find at the hardware store, with a touch of elegance thanks to the leather handles, these are baskets you'll want to make for every room!

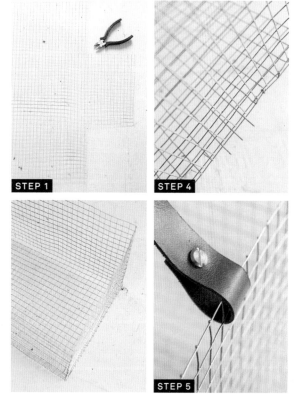

STEP 1

STEP 4

STEP 5

## HOW TO

### 1

Wearing protective gloves, cut the wire into a cross shape according to the size of the basket you want to make. The center will become the base, and the four flaps will be folded up to form the sides.

### 2

Cut the wire so that there's a straight edge all the way around, except for along the sides of two opposite flaps. You'll use these exposed wire ends to secure the sides.

### 3

Holding a ruler along the edge of the base, bend each flap upward until it's standing upright.

### 4

Using pliers, bend the exposed wire ends around the straight edge of the adjoining side flap on all four corners.

### 5

Cut a piece of leather for the tab and punch a hole in both ends. Fold the tab over the basket edge and use a screw stud to secure it in place. Add a leather hanger, if desired.

## YOU NEED

* Wire mesh, fencing, or flexible wire grid
* Wire cutters * Leather strapping
* Screw studs * Sharp scissors
* Leather punch * Basic toolbox (page 30)

The perfect kitchen
is a mix of function and
aesthetics. My tip is to start
with the function and how the
space works, then complement
it with decor that makes it
look and feel like you.

# Leather Wall Organizer

*Project*

Hanging space is one of the most underrated storage ideas for the kitchen. And although you might think that to take advantage of this you need a huge island with a gorgeous hanging pot rack above, you can get the same organizational effect with an unused wall. Why not create some great hanging storage for the things you use regularly and need at hand when you're cooking?

**STEP 2**

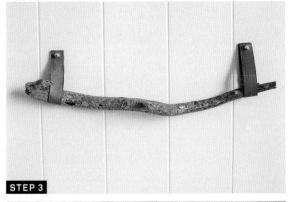

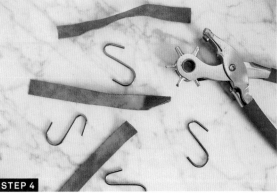

**STEP 3**

**STEP 4**

## HOW TO

### 1

Hammer two wall hooks or nails into the wall where your organizer will hang, spacing them so the branch or dowel has about a 2 in (5 cm) overhang at each end.

### 2

Cut two strips of leather about 8 in (20 cm) long. Punch a hole in each end to go over the wall hooks or nails. Fold the strips in half and push them onto the wall hooks or nails so that there are two loops hanging on the wall.

### 3

Hang the branch or wooden dowel on the wall through the leather loops.

### 4

Make the hooks by cutting lengths of leather strapping and punching a hole in each end. Fold each strap over the branch or dowel and insert an S hook.

## YOU NEED

* A branch or wooden dowel
* Leather strapping * 2 wall hooks or nails
* S hooks * Sharp scissors * Leather punch
* Basic toolbox (page 30)

# Painted Wooden Spoons

*Project*

Cooking is supposed to be a joy, but sometimes it can feel a bit tiresome. I've found that investing a little time in making beautiful accessories for my kitchen helps inspire my cooking. This project, while relatively simple to execute, is a great starting point for updating your kitchenware and the space itself. Think of it as the gateway to a complete overhaul!

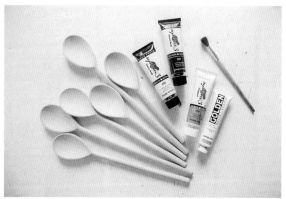

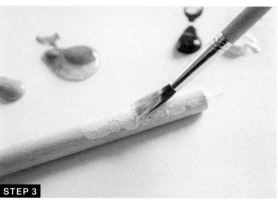

STEP 3

## HOW TO

**1**
Gently sand the spoons to remove any rough areas. Wipe away any dust with a damp rag.

**2**
Wrap a piece of painter's tape around the handle of each spoon to create a guide for painting.

**3**
Paint the spoons, using two coats of food-safe paint. Allow the spoons to air dry for at least an hour.

**4**
Place the dry spoons in a cold oven, then heat the oven to 350°F (180°C). Bake the spoons for 25 minutes, then turn off the oven and leave the spoons inside to cool completely. Wait at least 3 days before using the spoons. They should always be hand-washed.

Choose paint colors that complement the decor of your kitchen.

## YOU NEED

* Wooden spoons * Food-safe paint
* Painter's tape * Damp rag
* Basic toolbox (page 30)

# The Bedroom

*Make it a sanctuary*

# Time for bed!

And now, to one of my favorite rooms in the house . . . the bedroom! Before I get into the details of a great bedroom, it's important to first consider the purpose of the bedroom. Yes, it's where you get dressed or read a book. But at the end of the day, it's all about sleep.

I admit that, when I was younger, sleep was never high on my agenda—there was always too much to do and see. But as I've grown older I've come to understand that, above all else, getting enough good-quality sleep is the difference between a fantastic day and a terrible one.

When I first transitioned into working for myself, my sleep was awful. I often worried about my clients, and poor time management meant I was working late at night or waking at three a.m. Over time it wore me down and took a toll on my creativity and on my ability to think clearly. These days I subscribe to a fairly strict sleeping routine,

and it's completely changed my life. It's given me enthusiasm and creativity that I just didn't have when I was strung out from insufficient sleep.

One of the most important things I did to help make sleep a priority was to carefully consider my sleeping environment. My thinking changed from the bedroom being merely a place to lay my head to being an escape or sanctuary that looked beautiful but also helped to establish really good sleeping habits and routines.

So when you're considering your bedroom, think first about how the design and aesthetics can help to encourage better sleep, from your bed itself to light and ventilation. Also consider how the color scheme can help you feel relaxed. All of these can contribute to a great night's sleep. When your bedroom is a comfortable escape, a retreat from the outside world, you're more likely to be able to completely switch off and unwind.

When your bedroom is a comfortable escape, a retreat from the outside world, you're more likely to be able to completely switch off and unwind.

# Checklist for a Bedroom Sanctuary

Decorating a bedroom often happens slowly: you add a few things here and there, without ever taking stock of the whole space. This checklist will help you consider what you should include in your bedroom. Note that when it comes to creating your sanctuary, what's inside the bedroom is just as important as what's not. Ditch the phone, laptop, and TV, and opt instead for art and other items that create a soothing environment.

## ☐ A comfortable bed

If you're not getting enough good-quality sleep, you won't be able to appreciate anything else about the room. It's worth investing in the best mattress you can afford. Add some lovely bed linen, pillows, and cushions. The idea is to have enough pillows that your bed looks inviting, but not so many that you get tired of moving them around. I like using two European-style pillows and two smaller cushions.

## ☐ A nightstand

A beautiful nightstand is a functional item that will help create a great sleep routine. You don't necessarily have to have matching ones, and you can even use a chair, a chest, or a stool.

## ☐ Storage

Unless you have a separate space for your closet, storage in the bedroom is essential. A wardrobe or clothing rack is functional above all, but a dresser can be both pretty and useful. Top it with a mirror to add light to your room.

## ☐ A place to sit

Having a spot to sit down will serve you well when you're reading or just need to take a moment to yourself. A small bench is a great option (see page 64).

## ☐ Lighting

Lighting is incredibly important in the bedroom. In addition to your overhead lights, bedside lamps help you transition from bright lights to bedtime.

## ☐ A soft rug

Make sure your first step into the day is soft and warm—stepping onto a cold, hard floor is not a great incentive to get out of bed in the morning.

## ☐ Plants

I always include some soothing greenery in a bedroom. Instead of several plants, I often opt for a single large one.

## ☐ A personal touch

Once all the big pieces are in place, add a personal touch in the form of art, a wall hanging, or an alarm clock.

# Upcycled Nightstand Project

A nightstand is a place within arm's reach of your bed that holds everything you need to prepare for a perfect night's sleep. This easy and very inexpensive project uses an upcycled wine crate and just a few other materials to help you craft your own rustic nightstand.

STEP 2

STEP 3

STEP 6

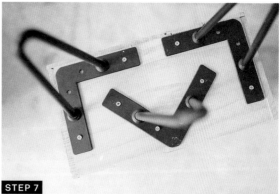

STEP 7

## HOW TO

**1**
Cut the plywood (or ask the hardware store to cut it for you) to fit snugly inside the crate to form a shelf.

**2**
Slide the shelf into the crate and mark on the sides of the crate where it will sit, then remove the plywood.

**3**
Drill two pilot holes on either side of the crate for the shelf to screw into.

**4**
Squeeze a line of wood glue along the edges of the shelf. Line it up with the markings.

**5**
Using the pilot holes in the sides of the crate as a guide, drill through the holes again, drilling right through into the shelf.

**6**
Screw the 1¼ in (3 cm) screws through the crate and into the plywood.

**7**
Mark the placement of the legs through the screw holes in the legs. Drill pilot holes, ensuring you don't drill through the base of the crate, then install the ½ in (1 cm) screws to secure the legs to the crate.

## YOU NEED

* Wooden wine crate * Plywood sheet
* 3 hairpin legs * Power drill * Wood glue
* 4 wood screws, 1¼ in (3 cm) long
* 7 wood screws, ½ in (1 cm) long
* Basic toolbox (page 30)

**Tip**

If your bedding colors vary with the seasons, it helps to keep the wall color neutral.

PERFECTING YOUR SPACE

# CREATING A GALLERY WALL

If there's one thing that injects personality into a room, it's art. Large pieces of unique artwork can completely transform a space, but can also sometimes be impractical or expensive to purchase. Another option for an art display that speaks volumes (without a huge cost) is a gallery wall. I love creating gallery walls as either the focal point of a room or a facelift for an empty corner that needs a bit of love.

 **DECIDE ON THE SPACE**

Obviously, one of the key elements of your gallery wall will be the space you use to display it, mainly in terms of the size of the wall. Don't feel you have to fill a whole wall; you can use a vertical or horizontal section only if that works better or if your collection is limited.

 **CONSIDER THE LAYOUT**

The types of frames and elements that you want to integrate will determine the best gallery layout, and whether the layout is symmetrical or more random. Rule of thumb: if you have similar-sized frames or identical pieces, go for symmetry; if you have more eclectic pieces, a random design will work better.

 **CHOOSE YOUR ART**

Collect all of the items you want to include in your gallery. Don't constrain yourself to art—anything flat can be framed. Get creative and think about using wrapping paper, maps, cards, or tickets. Think of it as the scrapbooking project that gets to see the light of day and reminds you of happy times!

 **CHOOSE YOUR FRAMES**

If you're going for a design where the art is very similar, you might consider choosing similar frames. If you're going for a more organic look, mixing frames also works. White, black, and pinewood frames work well together. Also think about whether you want to include white picture mounts inside the frames, which will give the art space to breathe and lend a slightly more sophisticated result.

 **ADD TEXTURE**

Vintage items like small wall hangings, rosettes, and other items with sentimental value can add texture and interest to your gallery wall, as well as adding a personal touch. These are best used when you're creating an organic or random layout.

 **PLAN YOUR LAYOUT**

It really pays to plan your layout. You'll be surprised how hard it is to create a layout you're happy with just by eye. One trick in the stylist's book is to cut out pieces of craft paper in the shape and size of your frames and move them around on the wall using tape until you find the perfect layout.

 **HANG YOUR ART**

One you've decided on the layout, methodically remove the craft paper and replace it with the art. I like to use 3M Command Picture Hanging Strips, placing a strip on the top and bottom of each frame. If you plan to hang your art by eye, it's a good idea to start with the biggest items. Remember that visually, less space between the art is better than more.

*Plan it out!*

White, black, and pinewood frames are a good mix.

# Gallery Wall Ideas

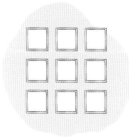

SQUARE BLOCKS

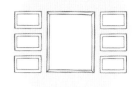

CENTERED

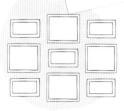

CHECKERED

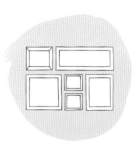

TETRIS

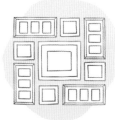

SPIRAL

MIX AND MATCH

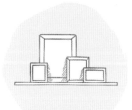

ON A SHELF

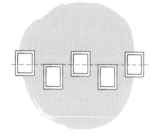

CHEVRON

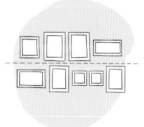

ALONG A LINE

READER'S DIGEST ATLAS OF AUSTRALIA

# Plate Wall Light

## Project

Creating a beautiful low-light environment is absolutely key to a space that helps you transition from a big day of work or study to feeling relaxed and sleepy. Bright lights from screens make it hard for our brains to recognize that we're tired. Having a light that you can read by but that doesn't keep you in an overly alert state is essential for the bedroom. Lighting projects can be tricky, but this one includes a clever hack that will make you want to experiment with lots of different styles.

## HOW TO

### 1

Using a glue gun, glue the battery pack from the lights onto the back of the plate, making sure the on/off switch and battery compartment are accessible.

### 2

Once the glue is dry, wrap the lights around the battery pack so that they are facing outward. Carefully secure the lights to the plate using a few dabs of glue.

### 3

Apply the Picture Hanging Strips to the battery pack. Follow the instructions to stick your plate light to the wall.

STEP 1

STEP 2

STEP 3

## YOU NEED

* A wooden or ceramic plate * String lights with a battery pack (check that the on/off switch is on the side) * Glue gun * 3 sets of 3M Command Picture Hanging Strips

Textiles, rugs, and lots of light come together to create a really beautiful bedroom space. Top it off with some personal touches for the ultimate escape.

# Simple Throw Pillow

*Project*

If you're looking for a project that packs the most design punch into the least time (and financial) investment, throw pillows are your best friend. I honestly think that throw pillows have a superpower when it comes to transforming a space and communicating the style or feel that you're going for—whether it be classic, boho, Hamptons, or anything else. If you've ever bought throw pillows, you'll know that they're often pricey, but given that they're relatively straightforward to make, you'd be crazy not to try!

## HOW TO

**1**
Using the dimensions of your pillow insert as a guide, draw a rectangle that's the same width of your insert, plus a ¾ in (2 cm) seam allowance on each side. The length of the rectangle needs to be double the length of your insert, plus 8 in (20 cm) for the slip cover and a ¾ in (2 cm) seam allowance on each end. For example, if you have an 8 x 8 in (20 x 20 cm) pillow, you'll need a 9½ x 25¼ in (24 x 64 cm) piece of fabric.

**2**
Carefully cut out the fabric rectangle.

**3**
Fold over and top stitch (or overlock) the short ends of the rectangle—these will be the opening for the pillow cover.

**4**
Fold the ends of the rectangle into the center, with the right side of the fabric inside. Overlap the ends for the opening by 4 in (10 cm) and pin the sides together. Sew down each side of the cover.

**5**
Remove the pins and flip the pillow cover right side out, then slip the pillow insert inside.

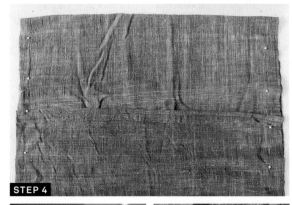

STEP 3

STEP 4

STEP 5

## YOU NEED

\* Heavy-duty fabric \* Pillow insert
\* Fabric chalk or pencil \* Fabric scissors
\* Sewing machine \* Basic toolbox (page 30)

**Reuse + recycle**

Look in
your local
secondhand
store for
fabric
to make
pillows.

## Ask Geneva

### HOW DO I STYLE A TINY BEDROOM?

**Q** I know that when it comes to bedrooms, big is considered beautiful—those giant spaces with enough room for a sofa at the end of the bed. What about small bedrooms? Can they be pretty, too?

**A** I'm no stranger to small bedrooms, but instead of looking at them as suffocating, I try to see them as cozy and relaxing. Choose comfortable decor and calming color palettes to emphasize this feeling; it's all about how you design and style the space to get the most out of it.

**Use the walls**
Don't overlook the walls in your room as a way to decorate—a creative headboard is a great place for a feature that doesn't have to take up much space.

**Pick the right bed**
Consider a bed with drawers underneath for storage so that you can minimize the amount of furniture you need in the room.

**Think about placement**
In a large bedroom, you'd probably put the bed in the middle of a wall, but this often isn't possible in a small bedroom. Try to make sure there's some room around the sides of the bed, even if it's only a tiny amount.

**Choose simple bedside tables**
No room for matching nightstands? Use small stools, hanging tables, or floating shelves instead.

**Use the bed as decor**
Cushions, linens, and blankets are all great ways to integrate texture and color into your bedroom. If put together in a cohesive way, they create a great theme.

# Brass Wall Hanging

 Project

When it comes to creating a beautiful bedroom, to me it's all about the personal touches. And what could be more personal than a wall hanging you've made by hand? I love the luxe feel of adding brass to the bedroom. This piece is perfect hanging above your nightstand or as a feature above the bed.

**STEP 1**

**STEP 3**

**STEP 4**

## HOW TO

**1**
Cut out your desired shapes from the brass sheeting using tin snips or cutting pliers.

**2**
Lay out the brass pieces along with the brass rod or hoop and move them around until you're happy with your design.

**3**
Rest each brass shape on the wooden block and use a hammer and large nail to punch a hole in the top (and bottom, if the piece is a linking piece) of each shape.

**4**
Attach the linking pieces together using the jump rings, then attach them to the rod or hoop.

**5**
Tie a length of cord to the top of the rod or hoop. Hang the wall hanging from a picture hook.

```
Making
templates
out of stiff
cardboard
will make
cutting out
the shapes
much easier.
```

## YOU NEED

\* Brass sheeting \* Brass rod or hoop
\* Small gold jump rings \* Cotton cord
\* Picture hook \* Tin snips or cutting pliers
\* Small round-tipped pliers \* Small wooden block
\* Large nail \* Basic toolbox (page 30)

# BEDSIDE TABLES

It's indisputable: a great bedroom has a nightstand that's filled with all the essentials to prepare you for a perfect night's sleep. Once you've got the furniture in place, take some time to style your nightstand so that it's not only functional but also beautiful. Here are some items you should consider including on your nightstand.

###  LIGHTING

No one likes stumbling around looking for a light switch in the middle of the night, so the first item to add to your nightstand is a lamp. It's useful to consider the scale of the lamp—it needs to fit the size of your room and your nightstand. The brightness of the lamp is also important. Personally, I recommend a lamp that's dim enough to calm you but also bright enough for reading. Or consider a simple wall light like the DIY one on page 140.

###  A TRAY

A tray might seem a bit frou-frou and frivolous when it comes to styling, but it actually has a purpose: it helps to corral all your bits and pieces and keep them from being knocked onto the floor. And the best thing for messy people like me? A tray helps make things look organized with very little effort.

###  A BOWL

Having a small bowl on your nightstand will also help you organize your nighttime and morning routines. It's a great place to hold small items like earrings, rings, and watches.

###  A CANDLE OR ESSENTIAL OILS

No bedtime routine is complete without a moment of peace, best created with the lighting of a candle or a little face massage with some lavender oil. Be sure to blow out the candle before you drift off to sleep!

Some dried
grasses
or flowers
are a
low-maintenance
alternative
to plants.

# Ask Geneva

## HOW DO I DECORATE THE WALL ABOVE THE BED?

**Q** I love my bedroom and have really enjoyed decorating it, but, for the life of me, I can't decide what to do above my bed!

**A** If there's one space that can confound me when it comes to decorating, it's the space above the bed. It should be interesting, but it also needs to pair well with your bedding and the rest of the room. If your room is feeling bare and empty, the open space above your bed might need some love. One important thing to note: when you're hanging anything above your bed, make sure you secure it really well using some heavy-duty hooks, particularly if it's heavy.

### Gallery wall

Gallery wall lover, right here! A gallery wall is a great idea if you have a big space to fill and want to create lots of interest (see pages 134–37). I love to fill a gallery wall with a mix of artwork and framed sentimental items. If you change your bedding often and the colors vary, it's a good idea to keep the color palette of your gallery wall neutral.

### Artwork

For something a little simpler than a gallery wall, opt for a single large piece of art. Play around with the size, depending on how much space you have, and consider how the art looks with the other colors in your room.

### Rug

A rug or large tapestry is a great textile to hang on your wall, and it's easy to change every now and again. One option is to run a curtain rod above the bed, which allows you to experiment with draping different textiles. Choose one that's narrower than your bed to ensure that it doesn't dominate the space.

### Mirror

I love the idea of hanging a mirror above the bed, particularly in a small space where it can also reflect light and make the room seem bigger.

### Hats

Chances are you have a few hats gathering dust, so why not turn them into art and hang them above your bed? If you use 3M Command adhesive wall hooks, you can move them around easily.

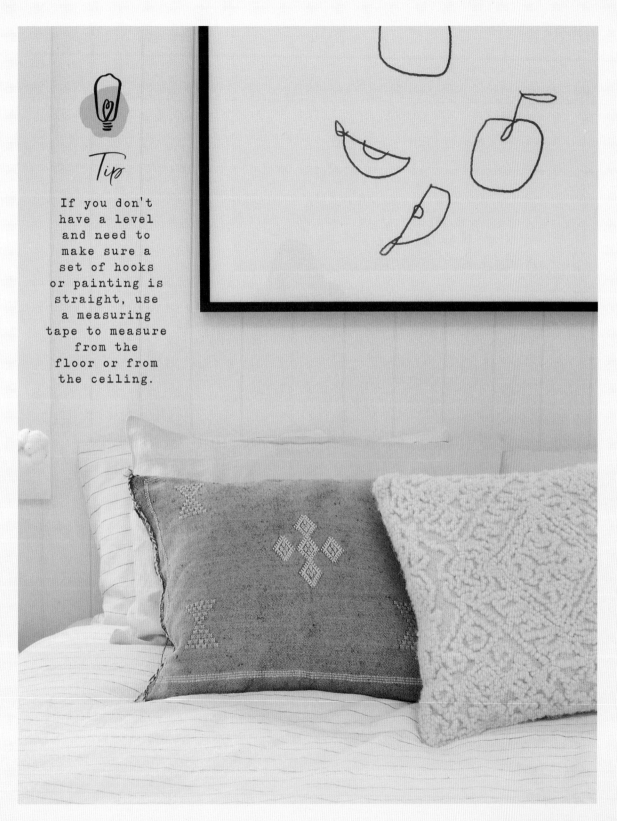

## Tip

If you don't have a level and need to make sure a set of hooks or painting is straight, use a measuring tape to measure from the floor or from the ceiling.

# The Closet

*Make it organized*

# A place for everything

If there's one space in the house that rarely gets the attention it deserves, it's the closet. Perhaps it's because most of us are unable to dedicate a whole room to being a closet, or because we see the closet as a storage solution rather than a location in its own right. Whatever the case, chances are your closet could do with a little bit of love.

I know from experience that an organized closet has the power to change your life—it really does! Being able to get dressed every morning without throwing yourself on the floor in despair is very important, and your chances of being able to do that are much higher if you have an organized closet. Not only will you be able to get dressed faster, you'll feel more in control of your life when you see an organized and accessible collection of clothing each day.

I admit to being one of the messiest people alive. However, I've learned the value of having a closet that doesn't look like your house has been ransacked. The trick is to create storage systems that actually work, as well as to get rid of anything you don't need. This chapter includes a bunch of amazing storage projects that won't overstretch your DIY skills. Most of the projects will also work elsewhere in your house, such as in the bathroom or bedroom. No matter their location, they're guaranteed to help you get organized.

# Checklist for an Organized Closet

Whether you have a big walk-in wardrobe or a tiny closet, there are a few essentials that every closet needs. This checklist will help you create a functional space where everything has its place, making it easy for you to get ready in a flash.

### ☐ Hanging space

This is a no-brainer, so whether you have a whole room or a tiny closet, make sure you have enough hanging space. Add rails inside wardrobes to give you more space, or a freestanding rack can do the trick. Maximize your hanging space by splitting vertical hanging spaces with a rail so that you have double the space and can hang shorter items.

### ☐ Drawers

Another essential in your closet setup is a few sets of drawers. I like to use a cabinet set of drawers that can do double duty as a simple vanity.

### ☐ Baskets and boxes

You'll be surprised how useful it is to have various baskets and boxes in your wardrobe. They organize clutter in an elegant way, and are ideal for stacking on top of cupboards or shelves.

### ☐ Shoe storage

I like to store my shoes on shelves where I can see them, but you can also store them in baskets, at the bottom of the wardrobe, or on a hanging shoe rack.

### ☐ Jewelry storage

I love creative jewelry storage! You'll see from the jewelry frame project on page 167 that jewelry storage can be just as pretty as the jewelry itself, and should definitely be on display.

You may be able to buy lengths of copper pipe in the exact sizes you need instead of cutting it yourself.

# Copper Pipe Garment Rack

*Project*

Hanging space has to be the most prized element of any great closet, and a little extra never hurts. That's why I love to include a simple rack like this one, either to act as a key part of my functional closet or as a place to deal with overflow or to help me plan my outfits. This project is incredibly easy to make, and will pack serious design (and function) punch in any closet.

STEP 1

STEP 4

STEP 5

## HOW TO

### 1

Ask the hardware store to cut the copper pipe to size. Otherwise, you can buy a pipe cutter that clamps onto the pipe and spins around to cut it.

### 2

To create the base, join two of the 24 in (60 cm) pipes together using one of the pipe tees. Secure them with the epoxy glue. Repeat this step with the other two 24 in (60 cm) pipes and the second pipe tee. Set aside to dry.

### 3

Glue a pipe elbow to each end of the 36 in (90 cm) pipe. Set aside to dry.

### 4

Glue the two 60 in (1.5 m) pipes to the two base pieces. These form the upright sides. Set aside to dry.

### 5

Glue the two side pieces to the pipe elbows at the ends of the long pipe. Set aside to dry before using.

## YOU NEED

* 4 x 24 in (60 cm) copper pipes
* 1 x 36 in (90 cm) copper pipe * 2 x 60 in (1.5 m) copper pipes * 2 copper pipe tees
* 2 copper pipe elbows * Epoxy glue

Tip

We DIYed these
built-ins
using kitchen
cabinets!

Hanging your hats helps keep them in shape. Just add some picture hooks to the wall.

# Ladder Hanger

Project

A ladder is a seriously versatile item for styling and storage that you can use in pretty much any room of the house. I find ladders particularly useful in the bedroom and the closet for the temporary storage of clothes and accessories. They're also helpful when you're planning an outfit, or for hanging clothes you're considering wearing. For this project I've developed a very simple method for making a ladder, without using any difficult woodworking techniques.

## HOW TO

**1**

Measure and mark where you want the ladder rungs to sit on each of the two lengths of wood. I placed them 14 in (35 cm) apart.

**2**

Cut eight lengths of leather strapping that are double the diameter of the dowels. Punch holes in both ends of each leather strap.

**3**

Using the markings on one of the lengths of wood as a guide, drill a pilot hole for one of the leather straps to screw into. Screw one end of the strap in place.

**4**

Place a dowel underneath the leather strap, fold the strap over the dowel, and mark the board through the hole in the leather. The dowel needs to fit snugly inside the leather loop.

**5**

Drill the pilot hole, then screw the second end of the leather strap in place.

**6**

Once you've attached all of the leather straps, slide the dowels into the loops.

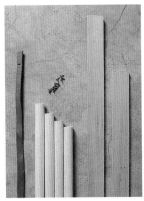
STEP 2

STEP 3

STEP 5

STEP 6

## YOU NEED

* 2 lengths of wood: 2 in (5 cm) wide by 64 in (1.6 m) long * 4 dowel rods: 18 in (45 cm) long * Leather strapping * Power drill * Sharp scissors * Leather punch * Basic toolbox (page 30) * 16 wood screws, ⅝ in (1.5 cm) long

Tip

For lighter
jewelry,
regular push
pins might
work, but the
long T-pin
stems help
balance heavy
pieces.

# Linen Jewelry Frame

*Project*

STEP 2

I often think what a waste it is to store gorgeous jewelry in a box, where you don't get the pleasure of looking at it. That gave me the idea of displaying jewelry like art, with this easy jewelry storage. You can mix and match the fabric to suit your decor. Go for a white or beige linen to keep it neutral, or opt for a pretty pattern for a pop of color.

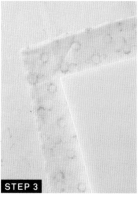

STEP 3

## HOW TO

### 1
Cut the fabric to the same size as the frame insert, adding an extra 1½ in (4 cm) on each side.

### 2
Cut the foam board to the same size as the frame insert. (If you're using thick fabric, you might need to trim the foam board a little smaller.)

### 3
Stretch the fabric over the foam board, pulling it taut, and use the glue gun to stick the four corners down. Work your way around the board, folding and gluing the fabric down as you go.

### 4
Insert the fabric-covered board into the frame, then add the frame insert and the backing.

### 5
Push the T-pins through the fabric and into the foam board, angling them downward for maximum hold.

STEP 4

## YOU NEED

* Fabric * Box frame * Foam board
* T-pins * Glue gun * Fabric scissors
* Craft knife

## Ask Geneva

### WHAT'S YOUR ADVICE FOR LIVING IN A RENTAL WITH NO BUILT-INS?

**Q** I just moved into a rental space, and the bedrooms don't have closets. I'm not sure what to do to create enough closet space without it all looking really messy.

**A** When we lived in London, we didn't have any closets, and it was quite a challenge. Luckily, there are a few hacks you can use to make life a little easier.

**Purge your closet**
This can be hard to take, but when you're dealing with a no-closet situation, it's important that you work only with the things that you love and actually wear. Take some time to go through your clothes and get rid of anything you're not sure about.

**Try a freestanding wardrobe**
You're going to need somewhere to hang all your clothes, and a freestanding wardrobe is a great option. You'll need to make a concerted effort to keep it tidy, but it will be useful to have. You can even make your own garment rack (see page 161).

**Embrace baskets**
For me, baskets are an essential for any space that lacks for storage. Slide them under the bed or put them in corners and on the top of cabinets. They're so useful!

**Utilize storage furniture**
Finding an ottoman or a bed that opens up for storage is a great way to reduce your clutter. It provides a home for excess towels, blankets, tablecloths, and duvet covers in a practical spot that doesn't need to be hidden away.

**Use the walls**
It's great to display your favorite items that you like seeing on a daily basis. I like to use the bedroom walls to display accessories like hats and scarves, and use shelves for displaying my favorite shoes.

**Store seasonal clothes**
At the end of each season, put away that season's clothes in boxes or a suitcase under the bed until you need them again. As you pack items away, consider donating any that you don't think you'll want to wear next year. Then, bring out the current season's clothes to hang in your standing wardrobe.

# Leather Tab Boxes

*Project*

You can never have enough boxes in your wardrobe. They're the perfect place to hide various not-so-cute items, such as socks or belts. This project is an easy update to inexpensive storage boxes. It's probably the simplest project in this book, but you'll find that it's a very useful one.

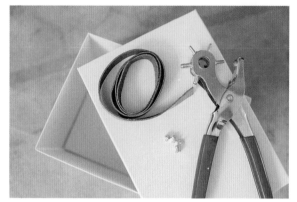

STEP 2

STEP 4

*Reuse + recycle*

Secondhand belts are a great way to repurpose materials for this project.

## HOW TO

**1**
Cut the leather strapping into two pieces measuring ¾ x 4 in (2 x 10 cm) and ¾ x 6 in (2 x 15 cm).

**2**
Using a leather punch, make a hole at each end of the leather straps.

**3**
Using a dart awl, make a hole in the middle of the front of the lid of each storage box.

**4**
Push the back of one of the rivet studs through the hole in one of the lids and one end of a leather strap. Fold the strap over and push the rivet stud through the hole. Hammer the rivet pieces together to secure the strap.

**5**
Repeat with the second box and leather strap.

## YOU NEED

* 2 storage boxes with lids
* Leather strapping * 2 sets of rivet studs
* Sharp scissors * Leather punch * Dart awl
* Basic toolbox (page 30)

# The Bathroom

*Make it a retreat*

# Spa inspiration

In most houses, the bathroom is the smallest room, and it often receives the least amount of natural light. Like the kitchen, it's often seen as being purely functional, but that doesn't mean the bathroom needs to be the most unloved space. We actually spend considerable time here, and there's nothing worse than a dark and depressing bathroom that you want to escape. I would know—I've lived with a few terrible bathrooms! However, I've always found that with a few small, inexpensive updates, any bathroom can be transformed into a spa-like haven that's a pleasure to be in.

When it comes to bathroom spaces that welcome relaxation and elevate my daily routine, I like to take styling notes from spa bathrooms that I've visited or seen online. And then there are the necessary functional features—adequate storage for everything from bath products to towels, lighting that serves the tasks performed in a bathroom, and finishes that are resistant to humid environments. That makes for a lot of goals for a small space, but they're absolutely achievable.

Even in the bathroom you'll find
me mixing old and new. This vanity
was an old sewing machine desk,
to which we added a basin and
minimalist tap.

# Checklist for a Bathroom Retreat

Want your bathroom to feel like you're visiting a spa? It's actually simpler than you might think. All you need are a few little upgrades or updates to make it feel like you're living large. Simple storage, sleek accessories, and elevated accents are the key to making your bathroom feel like you're staying in a hotel. As with any update to a space, it's a good idea to consider the theme and color palette first. For purely cosmetic updates, you simply need to make sure the textiles and decor tie in with the existing hardware.

## Clutter-free

A bathroom is a functional place, which is why so much clutter can accumulate. But if your bathroom is going to feel like a retreat, it's important to get rid of anything you don't need. Cull your items and keep only those you use. Hide items you don't want to be seen in a cupboard or drawer and display those that you like the look and feel of.

## Creative storage

Baskets are a great way to store towels out in the open if your cupboard space is limited. Use trays to group your beauty items and bring some order to chaos. Take the space up a notch by replacing packaging with jars or ceramics.

## Good lighting

It's a good idea to ensure the bathroom has a good source of natural light, if at all possible, as well as strategically placed overhead lights and a vanity or pendant light that shines on your face.

## Bath textiles

A few quality hand towels and bath towels really add a luxe feel. If you have limited storage space, use dead space like the back of the door to hang hooks or towel racks.

## Greenery

Greenery makes everything better! Add some plants to your bathroom, making sure you choose ones that will be happy with the light level (see pages 44–47).

## Mirrors

Mirrors not only provide a function in your bathroom, they're also good for creating more light and the illusion of a bigger space. Go for a mirror on the wall above the vanity, and consider adding a full-length one leaning against the wall.

## Accessories

Once you've got the functional items in place, add a few accessories such as fragrant candles and a soap dispenser.

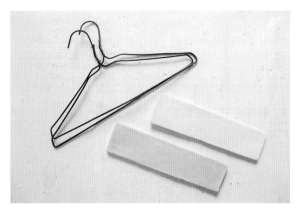

# Hanging Shelf
## Project

Marble is one of my favorite bathroom materials. If you live in a rental or don't want to do any larger-scale renovations, it's difficult to add marble to a bathroom. I really like this project because it allows you to inject a touch of marble easily and in a temporary way. And the best part is that basically all the materials can be thrifted or found for next to nothing—chances are you have a few spare metal hangers, and it's not hard to purchase or find a tile.

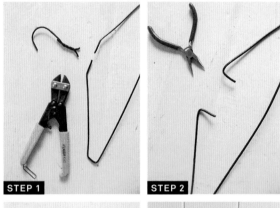

STEP 1

STEP 2

## HOW TO

**1**
Using cutting pliers, cut the hook off the coat hanger, pressing firmly and turning the pliers to cut the wire.

**2**
Use flat-nose pliers to bend the ends of the wire up at a 90-degree angle.

**3**
Pull the long side of the hanger toward you and bend it right at the halfway point. Straighten out the two sides.

**4**
Bend the wire ends to form the base of the frame. It should be just wide enough to hold the tile.

**5**
Paint the frame with gold spray paint. (If you're doing this indoors, set the frame in a cardboard box lined with newspaper and place it next to an open window.) Leave the frame to dry.

**6**
Add the tile to the frame and use a picture hook to hang the shelf.

STEP 3

STEP 6

## YOU NEED

* Wire coat hanger * Marble tile
* Gold spray paint * Cutting pliers
* Flat-nose pliers * Picture hook
* Basic toolbox (page 30)

You can
also use other
materials to
make the shelf,
such as wood or
terra-cotta.

## Ask Geneva

## HOW DO I STYLE A SMALL, DARK BATHROOM?

Q I've just moved into a new house, and the bathrooms are very dark and small. We're planning a full renovation in the long term, but in the meantime I'm looking for some quick fixes that will make the space better without spending too much.

A One of the most common issues with bathrooms is that they're dark and tiny. Bathrooms are often located in low-light areas and can have few (if any) windows, particularly if you live in an apartment or dorm room. They can be seriously depressing! Fortunately there are a few steps you can take to make the space feel larger and brighter.

**Go with a light palette**
One of the easiest ways to make your bathroom look bigger is to go with a white palette—white tile, white paint, white vanity, and so on. This tone reflects any available light to make the space feel bigger, and also naturally recedes so it draws your eyes away from dark corners.

**Use mirrors**
Add as many large mirrors to the space as you can. They will reflect light and make your bathroom seem bigger. A standing floor mirror is a great option, as are wall-mounted mirrors.

**Streamline storage**
Keep all of the storage flush with the walls, because anything that sticks out will make the space feel smaller. If you can, install medicine cabinets and recessed shelving.

**Get rid of clutter**
Nothing crowds a space faster than clutter. A good rule of thumb: if you don't need it there, store it elsewhere. Pare down what you keep in the bathroom to the bare necessities.

**Draw the eyes upward**
Add plants and artwork higher up on the walls to draw the eyes upward and create longer lines in the bathroom.

**Hide the bathmat**
Having open space on the floor makes a small bathroom feel bigger, so it's a good idea to put away the bathmat (perhaps by hanging it on the back of the door) when it's not in use.

When working with a tiny bathroom, avoid clutter and go for a light, bright palette.

*Reuse + recycle*

Simple mirrors are a dime a dozen in second-hand stores.

# Mirror Shelf

*Project*

This project combines so many things that I love for the bathroom—storage, a mirror, and a hanging element that allows you to move it around, depending on how you're feeling and how the room looks.

STEP 1

STEP 4

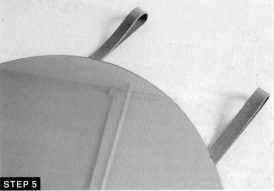

STEP 5

## HOW TO

### 1
Sand the edges of the plywood semicircles.

### 2
Nail the two straight sides of the semicircles together at a 90-degree angle, hammering a nail at each end and one in the middle.

### 3
Clean the mirror and shelf and let them dry completely.

### 4
Using a zigzag motion, coat the back of the shelf with Liquid Nails, then attach it to the mirror. Clamp the mirror and wood together. Leave to cure for 72 hours.

### 5
To add the hangers to the back of the shelf, cut two pieces of leather strapping to the desired length and fold them in half. Mark two equal points on the back of the mirror and attach the hangers using superglue.

### 6
To add the leather tabs, cut two pieces of leather to the desired length. Use the leather punch to make holes in both ends. Secure the tabs with brass studs.

### 7
Attach the mounting strips to the back of the mirror to help keep it level.

## YOU NEED

* 20 in (50 cm) round mirror * 20 in (50 cm) circle of plywood, cut in half * Leather strapping * 2 brass studs * 2 adhesive mounting strips * Liquid Nails glue * Superglue * Sharp scissors * Leather punch * Basic toolbox (page 30)

# Towel Holder *Project*

It's the little details in a bathroom that really help to take it to the next level. And not all the projects in your bathroom need to be difficult—it's incredibly easy to make a hand towel holder using a brass hoop and a leather strap. Instant spa style!

## HOW TO

 **1**

Fold the leather strapping in half, then use a sharp pair of scissors to cut two slits that are far enough apart to hold the brass hoop.

**2**

Decide where you want to hang the towel holder, then hammer the picture hook into the wall.

**3**

Fold the leather strapping around the brass hoop, then push the picture hook through the slits in the leather.

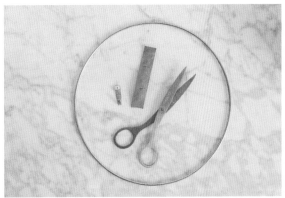

STEP 1

STEP 2

STEP 3

## YOU NEED

* Brass hoop * Leather strapping
* Picture hook * Sharp scissors
* Basic toolbox (page 30)

# WAYS TO ADD STYLE TO YOUR BATHROOM

 **ARTWORK**

Bathrooms often have limited wall space, so a giant piece might leave you feeling cramped. Consider adding something smaller above the toilet. You can prop the artwork against the wall if you're not able to hang it. Since there's the possibility of moisture damage in the bathroom, don't use anything precious.

 **A RUG**

Using a rug is a great way to bring warmth to the space. If you're lucky enough to have a freestanding tub, a rug will look great next to it. The texture of a rug can make the space feel more spa-like, and it's great to have something soft to walk on. Opt for a runner if your bathroom is narrow.

 **BEAUTIFUL BOTTLES AND JARS**

I like switching hand soap from store-bought bottles to recycled brown glass bottles with pump nozzles. I use a label maker to give them a little facelift. You might be able to find a low-waste store that allows you to bring in your bottles and fill them directly.

 **A STORAGE LADDER**

I love to hang towels from a storage ladder propped against the wall. You can make your own following the instructions on page 164.

 **A WOODEN STOOL**

A stool is a great functional item in the bathroom, but it can also add style to the space and house some of your favorite products or a beautiful plant.

 **A LUXE BATHMAT**

A rug might be controversial, but you'll definitely want to have a bathmat in your bathroom. They don't have to be ugly or sad-looking—go for light tones or patterns that match your bathroom.

# Beeswax Candles

## Project

Candles are a girl's best friend—who needs diamonds when you have candles? Candles create a beautiful ambience in any space and give the feeling of escape without having to travel anywhere. You can experiment with different fragrances to create your very own signature scent.

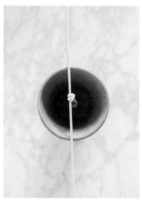

STEP 2

STEP 4
STEP 5

## HOW TO

**1**

Cut the wax into chunks using a knife and place them in a pouring pot. Bring a large saucepan of water to a boil, then hook the handle of the pouring pot over the side. The wax will start to melt over the boiling water.

**2**

While the wax is melting, slide a wick into a wick clip for each vessel. Using the wick stickers or tape, stick the wick to the base of each vessel. Place a wooden skewer across the top of each vessel and wrap the end of the wick around the skewer.

**3**

Once the wax is completely melted, whisk in 25 drops of your essential oil of choice.

**4**

Slowly pour the wax into the vessels, stopping about ½–1 in (1–2.5 cm) from the top. Let the candles cool for 24 hours to allow the wax to completely harden.

**5**

Cut the wicks down using a wick trimmer or a sharp pair of scissors.

## YOU NEED

* Clean vessels * Beeswax * Wicks
* Wick clips * Wick stickers or double-sided tape
* Lavender or geranium essential oil * Knife
* Pouring pot * Wick trimmer or sharp scissors
* Large saucepan * Whisk * Wooden skewers

## Tip

You can get
creative with
the vessels you
use for your
candles—try
glass jars,
vases, large
bowls, or even
terra-cotta
plant pots (with
the drainage
hole plugged).

# The Nursery

*Make it fun*

# A place to dream

There's nothing more fun than designing a nursery. As soon as I found out I was pregnant with Frankie, I was so excited about creating a concept for her room and DIYing all the little elements. Although it wasn't something I had thought about before, suddenly the idea of creating a tiny universe was very appealing! Once I started looking around for inspiration, I found it absolutely everywhere.

I wanted to create a space that would suit all the activities that would take place there, as well as inspiring a sense of fun and adventure. I wanted it to feel like Frankie's own little retreat, but also help her to imagine life outside those four walls. It was a very sentimental project for me.

Although designing a bedroom is fairly simple, I soon found out that designing a nursery is a whole new ball game. While it should definitely be a fun project, it's really important to think long-term when you're designing a kid's room. If you're not careful, you can design a room that caters to a very specific age and is stuck in a time warp. Redecorating every year might sound fun, but it's not really what you want to do, particularly if you have a few children! It really pays to plan out the decorating scheme and the furniture that goes in the room. In this chapter I'll share with you a few design ideas for creating an adaptable kid's room, and also some of my favorite projects for this special space.

While designing a kid's room should definitely be a fun project, it's really important to think about the use of the room in the long term.

# Checklist for a Fun Nursery

The best approach for designing a nursery is to tackle the basics, because you need a lot of functional items, and then turn your attention to the aesthetics. Chances are you'll spend a lot of time in this room, particularly when your baby is young, so you want it to be practical and comfortable, but also nice to look at.

## ☐ Crib or bassinet

The purpose of the room is obviously to be a place of rest for your little one, something that I'm sure you're hoping they like doing! When buying a bed or bassinet, it's important to choose something flexible and adaptable that can be reconfigured over time.

## ☐ Changing table

A changing table is essential, with a changing mat that reduces the chances of your baby rolling off. You'll also want some shelves on which to store all your changing supplies. And make sure that everything you need is within arm's reach, so you're never tempted to take a hand off your baby!

## ☐ Nightlight

When you have a newborn, with two or three feedings taking place each night, and the same number of diaper changes, you'll want to dim the lights so your baby doesn't wake up too much. Once your baby grows older, a nightlight can be useful for night wake-ups or even as something to help your child get to sleep. A light with a dimmer is perfect; IKEA has amazing dimmable light bulbs that you can use in a lamp.

## ☐ Seating

Whether you use a feeding chair or not, it's useful to include some seating in your baby's room for reading and for time out from play. I like a little love seat or armchair in the corner of the room.

## ☐ Storage

You can certainly accumulate a lot of stuff when you have a child! Consider adding extra storage to the nursery, including a chest of drawers, shelves, and hanging rails. I've found that having lots of baskets is very useful, both for keeping on shelves and for storing clothes, laundry, and other small bits and pieces.

## ☐ **Window covering**

Properly dressing your windows isn't just about design, it's important for safety, too. Install blackout curtains or heavy blinds, which will help baby sleep longer and more comfortably. Make sure you get the type that don't have cords.

## ☐ **Get DIYing!**

In the lead-up to the baby's birth, there's nothing better than getting crafty when you're feeling overwhelmed by what's to come. Shelving, canopies, little baby clothes . . . all of these are great DIY projects that are not only sweet but also help to calmly pass the time.

## ☐ **Add playful decor**

Finally, once you have all the essentials you need, it's time to add some playful decor. There are so many lovely things you can choose to bring some fun and personality—a rocking horse, maps on the wall, a rope swing, or a mobile.

# Beaded Shelf and Hanger

## *Project*

This pretty shelf is designed more for aesthetics than for functional storage. It's a little perch for your favorite items, especially any that need to stay out of reach. The hanging rail is perfect for displaying outfits that are just too cute to be put away.

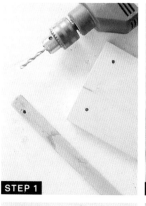
STEP 1

STEP 3

## HOW TO

**1**

Mark and drill two holes roughly ¾ in (2 cm) from each end of the wooden plank. Drill a hole at each end of the dowel, roughly 1¼ in (3 cm) from the end.

**2**

Thread one piece of cord through one of the holes in the back of the plank. Tie a knot to secure it.

**3**

String four beads onto the cord, then thread it through the hole in the front of the wooden plank so that there's about 6 in (15 cm) of cord beneath it. Tie a knot to secure the cord.

**4**

String another three beads onto the cord, then thread the cord through the dowel and tie a knot to secure it.

**5**

Repeat with the second side of the shelf.

**6**

Insert the picture hooks into the wall and attach the shelf, using a level to ensure that it sits straight.

STEP 4

STEP 5

## YOU NEED

* Wooden plank: 22 x 5½ x ¾ in (55 x 14 x 2 cm)
* 24 in (60 cm) dowel rod, 1 in (2.5 cm) thick
* 2 x 36 in (90 cm) lengths cotton cord, ¼ in (5 mm) thick * 14 wooden beads * Power drill
* 2 picture hooks * Basic toolbox (page 30)

The number and
size of beads is
up to you; just
make sure the
hole is big enough
for the cord to
fit through.
The more beads
you use, the
longer the cord
should be.

# Ask Geneva

## HOW DO I STYLE A FLEXIBLE AND ADAPTABLE NURSERY?

**Q** I love styling, but I'm a bit nervous about what to do in the nursery. I want it to be a themed space that will inspire imagination and fun, but I also want it to be a space my baby can grow into.

**A** You've stumbled upon every parent's decorating dilemma! I was tempted to get carried away with Frankie's room, but I always reminded myself that she will be in this space for years to come. Here are a few tips and tricks I used to create a space she'll love without going over the top.

### Go for neutral basics

In my experience, the best choices for bedroom furniture are simple designs in neutral colors. A fairy bed is great for a preschooler, but it will probably mean buying a new bed long before she's a teenager. Daybeds and oak wood are wonderful choices—they work well with any color and can be used for a child at any age.

### Spice it up with decor

Once you've got the basics in place, you can add some imaginative elements using pillows, textiles, artwork, posters, and accessories that give life and color. These items can be more age-specific, since they're easier to update.

### Choose simple wall colors

Keep paint colors simple for the walls so that you don't have to repaint all the time. I painted my childhood bedroom yellow and blue, and regretted it almost immediately!

### Maximize storage

Include as much storage as possible in the nursery. You'll be surprised how much clutter one child accumulates, even if you try hard to keep it to a minimum. Try to use all empty space for storage, such as under beds, on top of wardrobes, and underneath cabinets.

### Plan for updates

Although it's best to go neutral with paint colors on the walls, you should definitely experiment with paint colors elsewhere, such as on furniture, as this can be easily updated as your child gets older. And it's fun painting furniture together!

### Let the kids have a say

When you're planning a nursery, you can choose whatever you want; but as your child gets older you should start working together to plan the design. This will encourage your child's creativity and will help them be more engaged in the process.

Make this
floor cushion
in mud cloth
or any other
sturdy fabric.
I made this one
from a rug.

# Floor Cushion
## *Project*

Floor cushions offer the perfect, flexible solution for seating or lounging in any room of the house. They're ideal for increasing the capacity of a small space by allowing for comfortable floor sitting, and are perfect for a kid's room when friends come over or when you yourself want to sit on the floor and play games. This is one of my all-time favorite DIY projects. When you discover how easy it is, it's a project you'll want to make over and over.

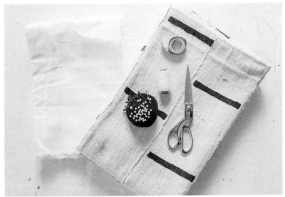

STEP 1

STEP 3

## HOW TO

**1**
Cut a 20 in (50 cm) square from the fabric for the top of the cushion. Cut four side pieces, each 10 x 20 in (25 x 50 cm).

**2**
Cut a 20 in (50 cm) square from the canvas for the base of the cushion.

**3**
With the right sides of the fabric facing together, pin the sides to the top square, then pin the sides together at the corners. Sew all the sides together.

**4**
Pin the canvas to the bottom of the cushion, leaving a gap on one side to add the beans. Sew the canvas to the cushion.

**5**
Fill the cushion with the beans until you're happy with how firm it is, then sew the opening closed.

STEP 4

STEP 5

## YOU NEED

* 79 in (2 m) heavy-duty fabric * 39½ in (1 m) square of canvas or burlap * Beanbag beans * Fabric chalk or pencil * Fabric scissors * Sewing machine * Basic toolbox (page 30)

# Rope Basket with Leather Tabs

*Project*

I confess that I have a bit of an addiction to rope. There's just something about the texture that I love, as well as the fact that you can use rope to make so many different projects. And it takes on such varying forms depending on the technique you use—there's really no limit to how many amazing things you can do with rope. In this project it becomes a basket that's perfect for storing toys or other small items.

## HOW TO

STEP 1

STEP 2

**1**

Start by wrapping the rope around itself in a spiral pattern, applying the glue every ½ in (1 cm). Continue wrapping and gluing until the spiral is the size of the base of your bucket.

**2**

Put the bucket on top of the spiral and continue winding and gluing the rope, using the side of the bucket as a guide. Be careful not to wrap the rope around the bucket too tightly or glue it to the bucket.

**3**

Once your basket reaches the desired height, take out the bucket. Trim the end of the rope and secure any stray ends with glue, then glue the end of the rope to your basket.

**4**

Decide on the length and position of the handles, then use the scissors to make slits in the sides of the basket. Thread the leather strapping through the slits and glue the ends in place inside the basket. Reseal the slits with some more glue.

STEP 3

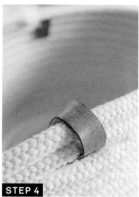

STEP 4

## YOU NEED

* 82 ft (25 m) cotton rope, ½ in (1 cm) thick
* A bucket * Leather strapping
* Glue gun * Sharp scissors

There's nothing I love more than creating a gallery wall in a child's room—a physical scrapbook that becomes a daily reminder of all the special times.

# Rope Swing
## *Project*

This rope swing brings a chic playground vibe to a kid's room and gives your little ones something fun to do in the room. Obviously, safety is very important, so make sure that you carefully install the swing in a suitable place and supervise children when they're swinging. It's a good idea to put the swing away out of reach when it's not in use.

**STEP 2**

**STEP 4**

**STEP 5**

## HOW TO

**1**

Sand the surface of the plank well, making sure it's very smooth to avoid any splinters.

**2**

Drill a hole in each corner of the plank, 1¼ in (3 cm) from each side. Make sure the holes are large enough to accommodate your rope.

**3**

Pass one length of rope through each hole on the shorter side of the plank. Check the length of the rope and trim it if needed.

**4**

Tie a firm knot underneath each hole and make sure that the knot can't be pulled through the hole. Unravel the ends under the knot to create a tassel effect.

**5**

Repeat with the second length of rope.

## YOU NEED

\* Sturdy wooden plank: 22½ x 9 x 1½ in (56 x 23 x 4 cm)
\* 2 lengths of sturdy rope, 16 ft (5 m) long and
⅝ in (1.5 cm) thick \* Power drill
\* Basic toolbox (page 30)

Install the swing
using ceiling hooks
that can support
265 lb (120 kg). It's
important that they're
attached to the joists
in the ceiling for
safety. Adjust the
length of the rope to
suit the height of your
ceiling as well as
your child's height.

# FRAMING MEMENTOS

Let's be honest, art can be a little bit stuffy at times, which is why I like to get creative with what goes on the walls in Frankie's room. Here are a few ideas for special items to hang on the walls, which you can adapt for other rooms in your house.

 **WRAPPING PAPER AND CARDS**

It seems a shame to throw out gorgeous wrapping paper or pretty cards. I like to reuse them by framing them and hanging them on the wall. I usually cut the pieces of wrapping paper to size and fit them into a frame. I mount cards on a contrasting colored piece of paper before slipping them into the frame. They're so easy to update, and they look great.

 **PAGES FROM BOOKS**

This is one of my favorite hacks for filling a frame and creating a statement piece without spending very much money or time. Simply tear or cut a page out of a picture book or vintage novel (the start of a chapter looks the best), mount it on a piece of paper, and then put it into a frame. If you want to personalize your art, choose a page that has a quote you like and underline that passage before framing.

 **MAPS**

As a child I traveled a lot, and I can't wait to nurture a love of travel for Frankie. I love the idea of a kid's room that inspires adventure and wanderlust. With this in mind, another great way to decorate the walls is by hanging up framed maps of places you've visited.

 **SENTIMENTAL ITEMS**

My penchant for creating interesting wall art knows no bounds, which is why I like to experiment with pretty much every sentimental item I own. Frankie's framed hospital bracelet has pride of place, along with old Polaroid photographs and other cute items. The sky's the limit!

Frame wrapping paper, cards, or pages from books for instant wall art.

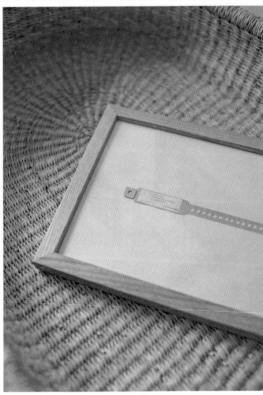

### Tip

Choose paper
that's strong
enough to
withstand
pulling down
and pressing on,
but not so thick
that it won't
roll easily
or tear off
when your
child is done.
I used 28 lb
kraft paper.

# Drawing Corner
## *Project*

I love the idea of a creative play space that a child can retreat to when they want to do some drawing. This easy-to-make drawing station is a great way to encourage a child to get creative, and is a practical design that's worth re-creating in other parts of the house, too!

**STEP 1**

**STEP 2**

**STEP 3**

**STEP 4**

## HOW TO

**1**
Thread the paper roll onto the dowel. Cut the dowel to size, if needed.

**2**
Cut two 8 in (20 cm) lengths of leather strapping. Punch holes in both ends of each piece of leather and insert the stud rings.

**3**
Decide on the height of your paper roll, then insert the picture hooks into the wall so that the leather loops sit about ¾ in (2 cm) from the ends of the dowel.

**4**
Thread the dowel through the leather loops, then hang the loops from the picture hooks with the paper roll to the front, so that the paper hangs flat against the wall.

**5**
Cut a piece of leather strapping that's slightly longer than the width of the paper roll. Secure it near the base of the wall with an adhesive strip at each end.

## YOU NEED

* Wooden dowel or curtain rod
* Roll of kraft paper * Leather strapping
* 2 stud rings * 2 picture hooks * 2 x 3M Command Adhesive Strips * Sharp scissors
* Leather punch * Basic toolbox (page 30)

# Resources

## FOR MAKING

**Etsy**
Etsy is a treasure trove for materials, particularly if you can't find them in your local area. etsy.com.

**Gumtree**
Gumtree is an Aladdin's cave of secondhand furniture and materials you can use for your projects. You can even set up alerts on Gumtree that will let you know if something you're searching for (say, a slab of marble) has been added. gumtree.com.

**Junk shops**
Many landfill sites have terrific onsite junk shops where you can get your hands on pre-loved items that have been discarded. You'll be surprised at what you find!

**Secondhand stores**
Thrift stores like Lifeline, Salvation Army, and other local shops often have a great selection of materials like fabrics, old furniture, and other items that are just waiting to be given a makeover.

**Bosch**
Bosch stocks a range of easy-to-use drills, from simple screw drills to larger, more complicated ones. boschtools.com.

**Black + Decker**
This is another great drill brand that I've used. blackanddecker.com.

**Singer**
I really like Singer sewing machines, as I find them very easy to use and perfect if you're new to sewing. Even their basic options will last for years. singer.com.

**Brother**
Brother is another brand worth considering if you're thinking of buying a sewing machine. brother.com.

**3M**
I love the range of products offered by 3M, including glues and other adhesives, and also their range of adhesive hooks and tabs for hanging projects. 3m.com.

**IKEA**
IKEA hacks are some of my favorite projects, and their basic items are ideal for updating on the cheap. ikea.com.

## FOR STYLING

**West Elm**
West Elm has fantastic furniture and furnishings that are made well and suit an eclectic style. westelm.com.

**Adairs**
If you're looking for great quality bedding, Adairs has an excellent selection. adairs.com.au.

**Etsy**
Etsy is a great source for all sorts of unique home decor items, and it's my go-to for affordable rugs. etsy.com.

**Jasmine Dowling**
I love Jasmine's art. As you can see from this book, it's perfect for styling. jasminedowling.com.

**Armadillo & Co**
This is one of my favorite rug brands; their rugs have such incredible feel and quality. usa.armadillo-co.com.

**Lumira Candles**
I'm a longtime fan of Lumira and their gorgeous candle designs. atelierlumira.com.

# Acknowledgments

First and foremost, I want to thank my community of readers across the globe. Never could I have imagined, when I started my website ten years ago, that pressing "publish" on my first post would lead to connecting with so many inspiring and creative people in every corner of the world. That I've been able to create a career out of making and sharing the things I love boggles my mind every day. I hope that this book empowers you to make a home filled with things you've made and people you love.

To the team at Murdoch Books, this amazing book turned out better than I ever could have dreamed, and it's all thanks to your support and kind direction. Kelly, from one crafter to another, it felt like fate when we met— thank you for believing that I could do this. To Madeleine, Justine, Jane, Vivien, and the rest of the team, you managed to shape my words and projects into this stunning volume, and I couldn't be more thankful. I hope we get to do this again and again!

To Ben, my ultimate supporter, your unwavering belief in my abilities has given me the courage to take the risks I have, and your patience in the face of my hundreds of questions every day deserves a medal. It's from you that I've gleaned so much practical and useful knowledge on the subject of interiors, and learned that perfection can be overrated. I couldn't wish for a better partner in crime.

To Lillie, Natalie, Nobel, and Terry, thank you for helping me bring together this book. Without you, it wouldn't have happened!

To Frankie, being able to see the world through your eyes has given me a reason to want to make a great home—not just a pretty one but one that's filled with adventure, play, and imagination.

To my mom, thank you for instilling in me from an early age the truth that women can do and be anything they want, and for creating in me a penchant for making do and making over. To my dad, your talent for inventiveness is the foundation for every time I ask myself, "Can I make that?" I'm lucky to have you both.

# Index

*Projects appear in italics.*

TILLER PRESS

An Imprint of Simon & Schuster, Inc.
1230 Avenue of the Americas
New York, NY 10020

Copyright © 2020 by Geneva Vanderzeil

Originally published in 2020 in Australia by Murdoch Books,
an imprint of Allen & Unwin

First Tiller Press trade paperback edition March 2020

TILLER PRESS and colophon are trademarks of Simon & Schuster, Inc.

For information about special discounts for bulk purchases,
please contact Simon & Schuster Special Sales at 1-866-506-1949
or business@simonandschuster.com.

The Simon & Schuster Speakers Bureau can bring authors to your live event. For
more information or to book an event, contact the Simon & Schuster Speakers
Bureau at 1-866-248-3049 or visit our website at www.simonspeakers.com.

Manufactured in China

10  9  8  7  6  5  4  3  2  1

Library of Congress Cataloging-in-Publication Data has been applied for.

ISBN 978-1-9821-4481-4
ISBN 978-1-9821-4482-1 (ebook)

Publisher: Kelly Doust
Editorial Manager: Jane Price
Creative Manager: Vivien Valk
Editor: Justine Harding
Designer: Madeleine Kane
Production Director: Lou Playfair

Text and photography © Geneva Vanderzeil 2020
Design © Murdoch Books 2020

Color reproduction by Splitting Image Colour Studio Pty Ltd, Clayton, Victoria

Printed by C & C Offset Printing Co Ltd, China

MIX
Paper from
responsible sources
FSC® C008047
FSC
www.fsc.org